In the Footsteps of Saint Clare

A Pilgrim's Guide Book

In the Footsteps of Saint Clare

A Pilgrim's Guide Book

Ramona Miller, O.S.F.

The Franciscan Institute
St. Bonaventure University
St. Bonaventure, New York 14778

1993

Copyright © 1993 by The Franciscan Institute
St. Bonaventure University
St. Bonaventure, New York 14778

All rights reserved. No part of this book may be reproduced or transmitted in any form or by any means, electronic or mechanical, including photocopying without permission in writing from the publisher.

All accounts regarding Clare are from *Clare of Assisi: Early Documents*, Rev. Ed. (ed. and trans. Regis J. Armstrong, O.F.M. Cap., St. Bonaventure, NY: Franciscan Institute Publications, 1993) unless otherwise stated.

All material from the early Franciscan Sources is taken with permission from *St. Francis of Assisi, Writings and Early Biographies*, English Omnibus of Sources for the Life of St. Francis, ed. by Marion Habig, O.F.M. (Chicago, IL: Franciscan Herald Press, 1973).

Illustrations by Clairvaux, O.S.F.
Tau Center
Winona, MN

Library of Congress
Catalog Card Number: 93–70664

Printed and bound in the United States of America by
BookMasters, Inc.
Ashland, Ohio

To Clare
and all Franciscan foremothers
whose lives enlighten our paths

The Sacred Places of Clare of Assisi

Contents

	Page
Illustrations	*viii*
Acknowledgments	*ix*
Preface	*xi*
Introduction	*xiii*
Abbreviations	*xvi*
Chronology for St. Clare of Assisi	*xvii*
The Family Home	1
The Cathedral of San Rufino	9
Perugia	17
The Portiuncula	27
Monastery of San Paolo	43
Sant' Angelo in Panzo	51
San Damiano	59
San Giorgio	83
Basilica of Saint Clare	93

Illustrations

		Page
1.	Family Home	xviii
2.	Cathedral of San Rufino	8
3.	Cathedral of San Rufino	12
4.	Perugia	23
5.	Portiuncula	26
6.	Investiture of St. Clare	28
7.	'Il Perdono' [The Pardon]	36
8.	Basilica of St. Mary of the Angels	38
9.	Chapel of San Paolo	42
10.	Sant'Angelo in Panzo	50
11.	San Damiano	58
12.	Ancient San Damiano	70
13.	San Damiano after Francis	72
14.	Monastery of the Poor Ladies	74
15.	San Damiano Today	78
16.	Mortuary Chapel of San Giorgio	82
17.	Basilica of Saint Clare	92
18.	Basilica of Saint Clare	94
Assisi		See foldout —inside back cover
Umbrian Valley		See foldout —inside back cover

Acknowledgments

Three Franciscan brothers—Francis, Bernard and Philip—accompanied Clare on her walk from San Paolo to Sant'Angelo. Three Franciscan brothers—Roch, Aaron and Murray—guided me as a pilgrim to the sacred places of Clare where she spoke to my heart. Beginning in 1987, as a staff member of the Franciscan Pilgrimage Program, I have the opportunity to accompany pilgrims each year to the sacred places of Francis and Clare. This Guide Book permits us to visit the places of Clare through an imaginative journey. The book would not have come about without encouragement from the staff of the Franciscan Pilgrimage Programs, the faculty at The Franciscan Institute of St. Bonaventure University, and the Leadership Team of the Sisters of St. Francis of Rochester, Minnesota. I also owe a debt of gratitude to three companions who daily journey with me and enlighten the darkness in my life: Ingrid, Margaret and Clairvaux.

Preface

"People long to go on pilgrimages," Chaucer wrote. "And palmers long to seek the stranger strands/Of far-off saints, hallowed in sundry lands...." How powerfully the words of our medieval English poet resonate as even we, pilgrims to Assisi, follow the ways of those who have come here before us, all of us involved in the challenge of discovering the ways of Francis and Clare and learning, perhaps, that we are no different from any pilgrim.

Thomas of Celano, Francis' first biographer, tells us: "[Francis] always asked his children to follow the laws of a pilgrim, that is, to gather under a strange roof, to proceed peacefully, to thirst for our homeland." (2Cel 59) We can certainly read these words on two levels: the human—those laws of a pilgrim are appropriate for any age; the spiritual—they speak deeply about our journey through life as we make our way to eternity. As we walk through the streets of Assisi and the fields and hills that surround it, we become aware that Francis himself is a perfect model of his own advice and reminds each of us of our pilgrim state. But Clare? How does Francis' perfect follower teach us this—she who lived in one place for more than forty years of her life?

This booklet is an attempt to answer that question. Page-after-page reveals the reflections of a pilgrim who was eager to learn from Clare, "the footprint of the Mother of God," as her biographer describes her. The story it tells looks at the Assisi of Clare rather than that of Francis.

"Is it possible to separate the two?" you might ask. Probably not. But, is it possible to separate Francis from Christ! Yet Clare teaches us, more clearly than any other, the wonder of Francis himself. "The Son of God," she writes, "has been made for us **the Way** (cf. Jn 14:6) which our blessed father Francis, His true love and imitator, has shown and taught us by word and example" (TestC 5). Clare learned from Francis the wonder of being a pilgrim walking in the footprints of Jesus.

Use this book well, fellow pilgrim. Learn from it what Clare teaches us all: look beyond her, look beyond Francis; look beyond to Christ Who points, as He did for the rich young man, to the One Alone Who is Good. As you proceed, pray for its author, all who have had a hand in it, and for all who share life's pilgrimage with you.

Regis J. Armstrong, O.F.M. Cap.

Introduction

Assisi sits comfortably on a foothill of Mount Subasio bordering the northern side of the Umbrian valley in the heart of Italy. The city situated on a southern slope dates back to pre-Roman times. Today you may see portions of the ancient Roman forum, which served as the center for commercial activity, by entering the area beneath the *Piazza Commune*. In the piazza, your eyes sweep over to the old Corinthian pillars of the Roman temple of Minerva. The temple still exists for worship—presided over today by the clerics of the Third Order Regular of St. Francis.

Many pilgrims find themselves transported back to medieval times when they first arrive in the valley below Assisi and look up to the "city on the hill." The natural contour of the skyline above Assisi is broken by the rebuilt feudal castle, the Rocca Maggiore. The feudal system crumbled at the beginning of the 13th century in Assisi when the citizens began their own local government, the *commune.* Simultaneous with the rise of the *commune* of Assisi was the birth of the Franciscan movement initiated by a son of Assisi, Francis. In 1209, Pope Innocent III approved the simple form of life that the Lord had directed Francis to choose for himself and his early companions. This "Rule and Life" that Francis believed that the Lord gave to him comes from three Gospel passages: "If you seek perfection, go, sell your possessions, and give to the poor. Afterward, come back and follow me" (Mt.19:21); "Take nothing for the journey, neither walking staff nor traveling bag; no bread, no money. No one is to have two coats" (Luke 9:3); and "Whoever wishes to be my follower must deny his very self, take up his cross each day, and follow in my steps" (Luke 9:23). Clare began the Second Order of the Franciscan family at San Damiano in 1212 with the advice of St. Francis. These two extraordinary persons, St. Francis and St. Clare, have captivated the hearts and imaginations of people for centuries. Their spirit sparks our desire, and that of every seeker, for deeper peace and more joy.

This book provides guidance to pursue the spirituality of Clare at the places where she lived and where her body lies. Four different aspects of consideration are provided for each place: 1) Clare's life experience at the place, 2) the historical background, 3) meditative reading, and 4) suggestions for further study. The readings provide background information and suggest sources for study.

Communing with Clare in the places where she lived opens us to a deeper understanding of the inner life that inflamed her heart. Her courageous exit from her noble home to a life of poverty at San Damiano has a timeless message for other Franciscans and for those who are yearning, consciously or unconsciously, to discover God. Walking in her footsteps in the Umbrian valley with an inquisitive imagination grants us the possibility of experiencing sensations similar to those which moved her to contemplation. Standing on the hillside viewing Mount Subasio, listening to the wind, feeling the heat of the sun and the coolness of the night breezes and viewing the sunset over Perugia leads us to gaze beyond the senses into God. Clare's mysticism was arrived at by a three-fold progression in prayer: gazing upon, considering, and contemplating God. As pilgrims who come to know Clare and follow her example, we will slow down, listen and gaze, and then arrive at the portal for mystical union with God.

The places that trace Clare's footsteps are sacred places, not just because they record her life–story, but because they hold the potential to be thresholds for our own transcendent experiences. A sacred place recalls past events of God's revelation at that site. Pilgrims visit such places to recall the history and to experience the spirit of the Holy that is specific to the place. At the same time, a sacred place holds the promise of future encounters with the Holy. Visiting sacred places in order to tap into their spiritual energies sensitizes our soul to a form of contemplative historical consciousness, the mysticism of the historical event. At a sacred place we recall its history not just as a memory–event, but as a movement toward a felt–experience of revelation at the site. To enter into the event of the past in such a way as to open ourselves to relive the encounter with God impels us toward the threshold of further revelation in the present moment, a new Epiphany. *In the Footsteps of Saint Clare* invites us to walk with Clare, who leads the way to a deeper intimacy with our Lord Jesus Christ.

Suggested Readings:

Armstrong, Regis J., O.F.M. Cap., ed. and trans. *Clare of Assisi: Early Documents*, Rev. ed. St. Bonaventure, NY: Franciscan Institute Publications, 1993.
Cousins, Ewert. "Francis of Assisi: Christian Mysticism at the Crossroads." *Mysticism and Religious Traditions*. Ed. Steven Katz. New York: Oxford University Press, 1983. 163-190.
Peterson, Ingrid, O.S.F. *Clare of Assisi: A Biographical Study*. Quincy, Il: Franciscan Press, 1993.

Abbreviations

BC	Bull of Canonization
BCl	Blessing of St. Clare
1Cel	First Life of St. Francis by Thomas of Celano
1LAg	First Letter to St. Agnes of Prague
2LAg	Second Letter to St. Agnes of Prague
3LAg	Third Letter to St. Agnes of Prague
4LAg	Fourth Letter to St. Agnes of Prague
Fior	Little Flowers of St. Francis
LegCl	Legend of St. Clare
LM	Major Legend of St. Francis by St. Bonaventure
LP	Legend of Perugia
L3S	Legend of the Three Companions
Proc	Acts of the Process of Canonization
RCl	Rule of St. Clare
SpPer	Mirror of Perfection
TestC	Testament of St. Clare

Chronology for St. Clare of Assisi

1193/94	Birth of Clare of Assisi
1199	Civil war in Assisi; Clare in exile at Perugia
1204/05	Clare returns to Assisi
1211	Francis and Clare have discernment meetings
1212	Palm Sunday night—Investiture at Portiuncula
	Holy Week at the monastery of San Paolo
	A few weeks at Sant'Angelo in Panzo, then San Damiano
1215	Fourth Lateran Council
1215/16	Clare becomes Abbess; receives Privilege of Poverty
1216	July 16th, Innocent III dies at Perugia
1219	Agnes departs for the new foundation at Monticello
1226	October 3rd, Francis dies
1228	Privilege of Poverty renewed by Gregory IX
1234	Clare begins correspondence with Agnes of Prague
1240	Saracens defeated through Clare's intercession
1241	Assisi spared through the prayers of Clare
1247	Innocent IV gives new Rule
1247-1253	Clare writes *Testament, Rule, Fourth Letter to Agnes*
1253	August 9th, Papal seal of approval for Clare's Rule
	August 11th, Clare dies
	August 12th, Clare's body placed in crypt of San Giorgio
1255	August 15th, Canonization of Saint Clare
1260	October 3rd, Clare's body transferred to Basilica
1850	Discovery of Clare's body
1872	Placement of Clare's body in newly–constructed chapel
1893	Discovery of Clare's original *Rule*
1986	Clare's body restored

Family Home

THE FAMILY HOME

Clare at her home

Clare's reputation for radiating the light of Christ began while she lived in her family's home, a residence of nobility situated in the upper area of Assisi. The Offreduccio house watchman, Ioanni de Ventura, testified:

> Although their household was one of the largest in the city and great sums were spent there, she nevertheless saved the food they were given to eat, put it aside, and then sent it to the poor. While she was still in her father's house, she wore a rough garment under her other clothes. He also said she fasted, prayed, and did other pious deeds, as he had seen; and that it was believed she had been inspired by the Holy Spirit from the beginning.   [Proc XX, 3a,4-5]

Clare's penitential life was noticeably different from the expectations that the society had for young noble ladies. The neighbors and townsfolk were cognizant that this beautiful woman was someone very special:

> The Lady Clare loved the poor very much and all the citizens held her in great veneration because of her good manner of life. [Proc I, 3]

Clare's reputation reached Francis who "heard of the fame of her holiness" (Proc XII,2). Could it be that he sought her out to assist him in accomplishing the dream of rebuilding the Church? According to Clare's own sister, Beatrice, Francis came to Clare:

> Francis went many times to preach to her[Clare], so that the virgin Clare acquiesced to his preaching, renounced the world and all earthly things, and went to serve God as soon as she was able. [Proc XII, 2]

Clare's spiritual journey had begun in her own home and her deeds indicated that she had chosen to live as a penitent: performing personal ascetical practices, prayer and acts of charity, especially making contributions of money and food to the poor. Francis' spiritual direction spiraled her journey out into greater ecclesial dimensions.

Clare's exodus from her home and the Offreduccio household took place at night, the night of Palm Sunday, 1212. She departed by way of a barricaded door that is sometimes referred to as the "Door of the Dead." In the Middle Ages many of the Assisi homes often had a concealed entrance separate from their main first floor door for security reasons. The custom of carrying corpses out through such doors gave them the title, "Door of the Dead." Clare's determination and strength of conviction that empowered her to leave her noble status became manifested in the physical energy she exerted during her departure:

> Because she did not want to leave through the usual exit, fearing her way would be blocked, she went out by the house's other exit which had been barricaded with heavy wooden beams and an iron bar so it could not be opened even by a large number of men. She alone, with the help of Jesus Christ, removed them and opened the door. On the following morning, when many people saw that door opened, they were somewhat astonished at how a young girl could have done it. [Proc XIII, 1]

Historical Background

The testimony of Pacifica situates the birthplace of Clare adjacent to the piazza of San Rufino:

> Sister Pacifica de Guelfuccio of Assisi, a nun of the monastery of San Damiano, said under oath she knew Saint Clare while that holy woman was in the world in her father's house; ...she [Pacifica] responded that when she was in the world she was her neighbor and distant relative and that only the piazza was between her house and that of the virgin Clare. She frequently conversed with her. [Proc I, 1-2]

Ioanni de Ventura gave an account of Clare's noble origin and a description of her home:

> Lady Clare...of the most noble stock of all Assisi, on both her father's and mother's side. Her father was called Favarone and her grandfather Offreduccio de Bernardino...their household was one of the largest in the city and great sums were spent there. [Proc XX, 2-3]

According to the Acts of Assisi, the most distant ancestor of Clare was Offredo—her great-great-grandfather—who lived in Assisi in 1106 with his sons Bernard and Monaldo. From this evidence, there have been efforts made to trace the family lineage on both sides back to Charlemagne. Clare's father, Favarone, son of Count Offreduccio, was a feudal knight who fought on horseback and pursued the enemy with a drawn sword. Clare's mother, Ortulana, had been born and raised in Assisi but had traveled a great deal on pilgrimages to Rome, the Holy Land and Monte Gargano.

Clare's name means light. She received this name because of a prophecy which her mother, Ortulana, enjoyed before Clare's birth:

> Lady Clare told the sisters how her mother, when she was carrying her, went into the church. While standing before the cross and actually praying for God to help and protect her during the danger of childbirth, she heard a voice telling her: "You will give birth to a light that will shine brilliantly in the world." [Proc III, 28]

The papal proclamation of Clare's canonization (1255) capitalizes upon the symbolism of her name that is synonymous with light:

Clare, shines **brilliantly: brilliant** by her **bright** merits, by the **brightness** of her great glory in heaven, and by the **brilliance** of her sublime miracles on earth. Clare, her strict and lofty way of religious life **radiates** here on earth, while the magnitude of her eternal rewards **glows** from above and her virtue begins **to dawn** upon all mortal beings... [BC, 2]

Clare was a young girl when it was necessary for her family to flee from their home in Assisi. For a few years they lived in exile with relatives at Perugia. When it was safe to return, her family resumed residence at their home in Assisi. Today, Sisters who serve as sacristans and pastoral workers live in what was the Offreduccio residence adjacent to the tower, on your right when you exit the Cathedral.

Further Reflection

Clare's zeal for evangelical perfection led her to leave her family and the security of her noble household because she desired to live a more radical response to the Gospel than was possible in her family's home. In 1212, Clare was attracted to Francis' way of life, a life of absolute poverty motivated by the love of the poor and humble Christ. The brothers' literal interpretation of the Gospel--especially the passages of their rule and life such as "Take nothing for your journey"--expressed total dependence on God. Their itinerant lives reflected their understanding of St. Peter's teaching that Christians are "pilgrims and strangers in this world" [1Pt.2:11]. Francis' first companions appeared as vagabonds witnessing that their lifestyle led them into a deeper intimacy with the Lord who blessed them with joy and with a wisdom they revealed in their preaching.

When Clare heard Francis preach at the Cathedral, she was already living a penitential life and had renounced marriage in order to fix her gaze on the Lord. Her desire to devote her life to God resonated with accounts of others who had left everything in order to join Francis. Clare wanted to abandon herself to this same radical lifestyle of absolute poverty, so she sold her part of the family inheritance in order to give the proceeds to the poor; then she left home to join Francis' movement.

> [Clare] desired to make of her body a temple for God alone and strove by her virtue to be worthy of marriage with the great King. Then she committed herself thoroughly to the counsel of Francis, placing him, after God, as the guide of her journey. Her soul relied on his sacred admonitions and received whatever he said of the good Jesus with a warm heart. She was already troubled by the tinsel of an ornate world and considered as almost dung everything acclaimed by the world, in order that she might be able to gain Christ (cf. Phil 3:8).
>
> [LegCl 6b]

Was it necessary for Clare to "leave home" in order to become holy?   Why?

What might this suggest for our lives?

Suggested Reading

Fortini, Gemma. "The Noble Family of St. Clare of Assisi." *Franciscan Studies* 42/20 (1982): 48-65.

Stewart, Robert M. "Francis' Conversion and Life of Penance." *"De Illis Qui Faciunt Penitentiam"*. Rome: Instituto Storico dei Cappuccini, 1991. 123-34.

van Leeuwen, Bertulf. "Clare, Abbess of Penitents." *Greyfriars Review* 4/2 (1990): 73-82.

Cathedral of San Rufino

The Cathedral of San Rufino

Clare at San Rufino

Clare's living faith was born in her through the saving waters of Baptism received at the baptismal font in the Cathedral of San Rufino. By the sacramental anointing, she became a daughter of God and an heiress to all divine riches. Her life demonstrated a blossoming of the spiritual inheritance that all baptized receive:

> For if you live according to the flesh, you will die, but if by the Spirit you put to death the deeds of the body, you will live. For those who are led by the Spirit of God are children of God. For you did not receive a spirit of slavery to fall back into fear, but you received a spirit of adoption, through which we cry, "Abba! Father!" The Spirit itself bears witness with our spirit that we are children of God, and if children, then heirs, heirs of God and joint heirs with Christ, if only we suffer with him so that we may also be glorified with him.
> [Rom 8:13-17]

Clare was a young adolescent when she heard Francis preach the Word of God from the Cathedral pulpit. Her heart was already responsive to the Spirit whose indwelling began in Baptism; her penitential life in her home displayed her loving response to the Spirit at work in her life. Like the Beguines of her time, she lived dedicated to prayer and good works. Francis' words inflamed the ardor of her love and she longed to live the Gospel more intensively. His preaching, asserts Lord Ugolino, led her to seek a new way of living:

> The virgin, Saint Clare, entered Religion at the preaching of Saint Francis and his admonition.
>
> [Proc XVI,3]

Sister Amata told of Francis' influence on Clare:

> She [Amata] knew her [Clare's] manner of life and had heard how she had been converted: through the exhortation and preaching of Saint Francis, she had assumed religious life, even though before she entered it she was considered holy by all who knew her because of the many graces and virtues the Lord had given her, as it was known about her through her reputation.
>
> [Proc IV,2]

Francis and Clare had meetings over a period of time until the discernment was reached, as the unknown author of Clare's *Legend* asserts:

> The father Francis told her that on the day of the feast [Palm Sunday], she should go, dressed and adorned,

together with the crowd of people, to (receive) a palm, and, on the following night, leaving the camp [Heb.13:13] she should turn her worldly joy into mourning [Ja 4:9] the Lord's passion. Therefore, when Sunday came, the young girl, thoroughly radiant with festive splendor among the crowd of women, entered the church with the others. Then something occurred that was a fitting omen: as the others were going [to receive] the palms, while Clare remained immobile in her place out of shyness, the Bishop, coming down the steps, came to her and placed a palm in her hands. On that night, preparing to obey the command of the saint, she embarked upon her long desired flight with a virtuous companion. [LegCL 7]

There is no indication that Clare ever saw the interior of the Cathedral after that Palm Sunday exodus. Later that evening, she walked to the Portiuncula for her consecration to religious life as the first Franciscan woman.

Historical Background

The early Christian community in Assisi built the first church of San Rufino on an ancient Roman temple site, a temple dedicated to "Good Mother." A sermon by St. Peter Damien (+1072) on the occasion of the translation of the body of Saint Rufino to a newly constructed altar at the beginning of the 11th century provides the source of dating the cult of Saint Rufino to the 3rd

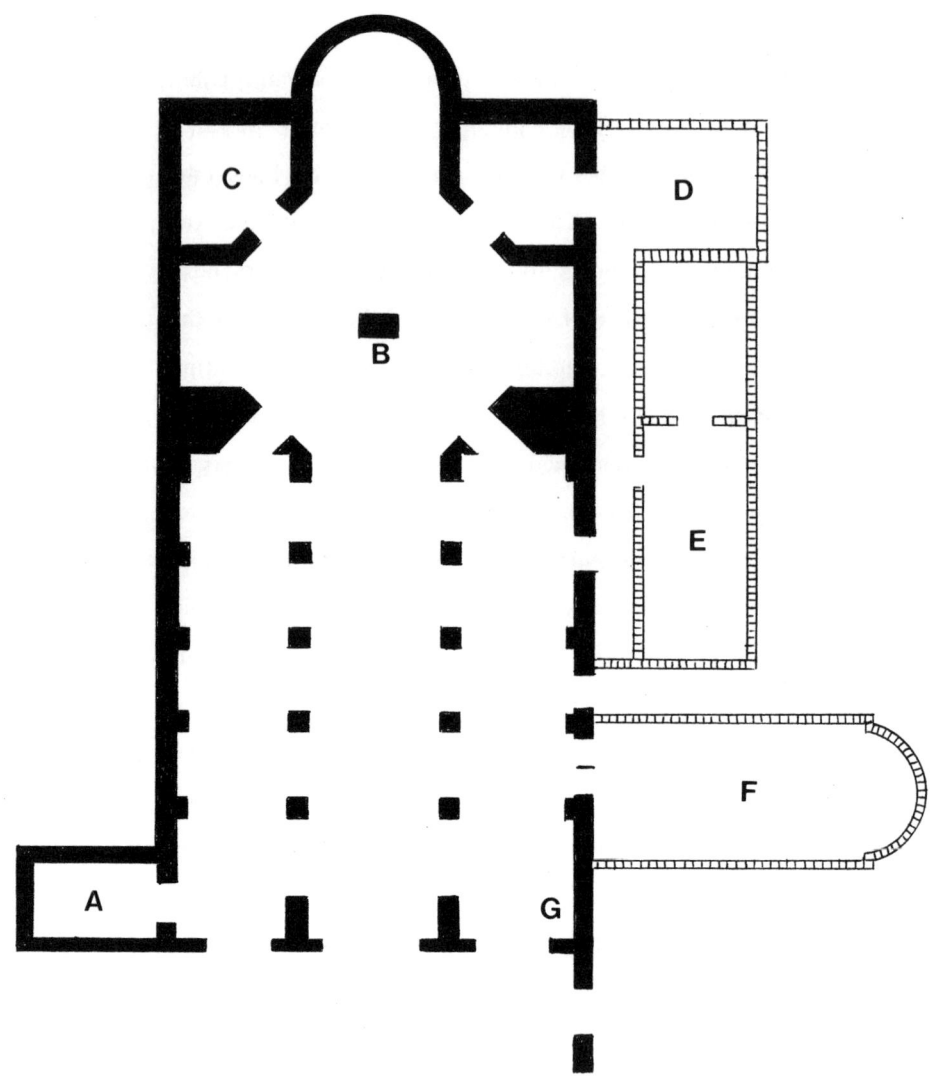

Cathedral of San Rufino

A. Roman Cistern
B. Main Altar
C. Chapel of the Weeping Madonna
D. Sacristy
E. Museum
F. Blessed Sacrament Chapel
G. Baptismal Font

century. According to this sermon, the relics of Saint Rufino, the first bishop of Assisi, martyred about 238 A.D., were placed under the altar for veneration. In 1148, a consortium of noble families in the upper part of Assisi, including Clare's grandfather, Offreduccio, gave the land for erecting a larger church to honor the saint and to display their faith in a fitting way. The nobility succeeded in building a grand basilica dedicated to Saint Rufino. Because devotion to him was so great, the basilica eventually gained the status of a cathedral, shifting the bishop's liturgical chair from the Church of Santa Maria Maggiore. However, the bishop's residence remained adjacent to the Church dedicated to our Lady.

Today, we may still approach the cathedral baptismal font which holds the honor of being the site for the baptisms of the notable saints, Francis and Clare, and other famous personages such as Frederick II. Francis was invited to preach at the Cathedral soon after Innocent III had confirmed his way of life and given him the mandate, "...as the Lord will inspire you, preach penance to all" (1Cel 33). A small oratory beneath the sacristy commemorates Francis' nightly prayer vigils before he would ascend the pulpit to proclaim the Word of God. It was here that he was praying when his soul visited the friars at Rivo Torto (cf. LM IV,4). The Cathedral was still in the final stages of reconstruction during the lifetimes of Francis and Clare; the main altar was consecrated by Gregory IX when he came to Assisi for the canonization of Francis in 1228.

The Madonna Chapel highlights the Assisians' Marian devotion. We can see a precious "Pieta," a replica of the statue that was seen to be weeping on the 6th of April in 1494 during fratricidal feuding. Mary's tears caused the citizens to stop their violence to each other at that time. In this century, Assisians have remembered those who have been killed in wars through plaques on the chapel walls. The bronze plaque on the north wall of the chapel commemorates the beloved Bishop Nicolini (+1973) whose generosity to the poor and the refugees during World War II will always be remembered.

Toward the end of the sixteenth century the interior of the Cathedral was entirely rebuilt in Doric style. The vault was reconstructed at a much lower level than the original roof, hiding two side rose windows--the center rose window dates from 1140. The baroque Blessed Sacrament Chapel was built in 1663 by the canons of the Cathedral and the local nobility.

Further Reflection

The Cathedral of San Rufino represents Clare's initial relationship with God: here she was baptized and here she was nurtured by the Word of God through proclamation and preaching. Francis' inspired preaching inflamed the heart of Clare and influenced her to make a radical choice to live totally for God. Toward the end of her life, Clare reflected upon her vocation:

> Among the other gifts that we have received and do daily receive from our benefactor, **the Father of mercies** (2Cor.1:3), and for which we must express the deepest thanks to the glorious Father of Christ, there is

our vocation, for which, all the more by way of its being more perfect and greater, do we owe the greatest thanks to Him.   [TestC 2-3]

God reached out attracting Clare: Clare responded. The exchange of love generated a deeper and ongoing desire within Clare to "run and never tire" (4LAg 31) toward the eternal embrace awaiting her. Clare's name for God, *Father of mercies,* indicates more than a familiarity with St. Paul. She grasped the meaning of a God whose heart's sensitivity to children's suffering and sorrow knows no boundaries. Clare's gratitude for the outpouring of such merciful love--a love that makes her tender as a mother for her sisters and a love that strengthens her as a father providing leadership--moves her to recall all the gifts she has received, particularly her vocation. According to Sister Filippa, when Clare was dying she was mindful of reflecting on her baptism:

> The witness [Filippa] added the whole night of that day during which she passed from this life, she admonished her sisters by preaching to them. At the end she made such a beautiful and good confession that the witness had never heard anything like it. She made this confession because she doubted that she had not offended in some way the faith promised at her baptism.
>
>   [Proc I,23]

How might our lives reflect gratitude for our Baptism?

Suggested Reading

Bonaventure, St. "The Life of Francis." *Bonaventure.* Trans. Ewert Cousins. New York: Paulist Press, 1978. 209-10.

Fortini, Arnaldo. *Francis of Assisi.* Trans. Helen Moak. New York: Crossroad, 1981. 33-37.

Godet, Jean Francois. *Clare of Assisi: A Woman's Life.* Chicago: Haversack, 1991.

McKelvie, Roberta A. "Clare's Conversion: A Counter-Cultural Choice." *Cord* 41/7 (1991): 202-07.

Perugia

Clare in Perugia

Clare arrived in Perugia as a child with her refugee family who had to flee Assisi because of warring in the streets between the nobility and the merchant class. Arnaldo Fortini describes the Offreduccio exile:

> As the war flared up, all of Clare's family took refuge in Perugia, where her uncle Monaldo had taken citizenship, according to the terms imposed on the knights who had committed themselves to fight against Assisi. The wrath of the people over this move exploded in an attack on the family house on the Piazza San Rufino, and it was severely damaged. In Perugia, Clare lived in the house of a girl who would become one of her first companions, Benvenuta.
>
> [*Francis of Assisi*, 333]

Clare was a young girl when her family took refuge at her uncle's castle near Perugia. The life within the noble household provided Ortulana the opportunity to educate her daughters: Clare, Catherine [Agnes] and Beatrice. This mother had been a well-traveled woman whose accounts of pilgrimages to the Holy Land, Monte Gargano and Rome supplied many stories for the formation in faith of her children.

> From the mouth of her mother she first received with a docile heart, the fundamentals of the faith and, with the Spirit inflaming and molding her interiorly, she became known as a most pure vessel, a vessel of graces.
>
> [LegCl 3]

Significant friendships sprang up among the young women who were under the tutelage of Ortulana during those years. Two of the women--Benvenuta and Filippa--joined the community of Poor Ladies at San Damiano after Clare and Agnes had moved into that place. Benvenuta testified:

> She, the witness, had known her before she entered religion and had stayed with her in [the same] house. From the time she entered religion, she stayed with her until her death, for almost forty-two years, except for the aforesaid time, that is, from Holy Monday until the end of September.   [Proc II, 2]

Benvenuta joined Clare at San Damiano at the end of September of 1212 and therefore knew her very well. Another childhood friend, Filippa, was the third to join Clare and she likewise gave an account that she knew Clare from her childhood [Proc III,8]. Rufino was Clare's cousin whose shared life experience in Perugia also matured into a Franciscan vocation. Rufino joined Francis in 1210 and was one of his favorite companions. He, like his cousin Clare, was a contemplative. Tradition maintains that he had a hermit's cave at the Carceri. In 1244, when Crescentius requested that friars submit whatever they knew of certainty about the life and signs and wonders of Blessed Francis, Rufino, along with Angelo and Leo, responded by gathering material and submitting it with a cover letter. This information is invaluable since these three companions were eye witnesses to the many stories of God's spirit at work in Francis. Perhaps Clare and Rufino reinforced each other's fervor as they recounted all that had happened along the way.

Relationships provided Clare with an authenticity for teaching others about family bondedness with Christ. In her first letter to Agnes of Prague, she wrote:

> Therefore, most beloved sister, or should I say, Lady, worthy of great respect: because You are the **spouse and the mother and the sister** of my Lord Jesus Christ [cf.2 Cor.11:2; Mt.12:50]...be strengthened in the holy service which you have undertaken out of a burning desire for the Poor Crucified. [1LAg 12-13]

Historical Background

As they watch the sun set, Assisians view the skyline of Perugia on the western rim of the Umbrian valley. Perugia was an ancient Etruscan city that fell to the Romans in 295 B.C. Etruscan engineering skills remain visible today at the base of the gateway, Porta Augusta, where huge blocks of travertine can be seen supporting its base structure. The griffin, a symbol of the warlike spirit of the city which would rise to any challenge of its power, appears on the city's banner. According to the legend, the griffin--an amphibian with a menacing beak, outspread wings and extended claws ready to tear--was a terrifying wild beast that was captured and killed by the Perugians on a nearby mountain. Perugia fluctuated in fidelity during the early Middle Ages from loyalty to the Duchy of Spoleto to membership in the Tuscan league. The dawn of its strong allegiance to the papacy began during Innocent III's reign. He, and popes after him, came to stay at the well-fortified city atop a hill which provided coolness in summer's heat and security amidst loyal citizens. The popes and visiting officials stayed at the "Canonica," a residence for the cathedral canons which adjoins the cathedral. St. Clare received her Privilege of Poverty from Pope Innocent III. Perhaps she herself approached the pontiff while he resided at the Canonica.

Francis was taken prisoner when the Perugians defeated Assisi at the Battle of Collestrada in 1202. The twenty-year-old Francis was with the captured Assisians incarcerated in the center of the city at a spot where the City Hall now stands. After a few months, Francis was released to return to Assisi. Years later, Francis' early companions told the following story of his return to that same piazza:

> One day when blessed Francis was preaching in the public square of Perugia before a huge gathering of people, some knights began to gallop there in full armor,

for the sport of it, so much so that they interfered with the sermon. The men and women who were listening attentively to the sermon protested, but to no avail; the knights continued. Turning toward them, blessed Francis said to them with all the ardor of his soul: "Listen and retain well what the Lord announces to you through the mouth of his servant. And do not say: Nonsense, he's a man from Assisi! (Blessed Francis spoke that way because a great hatred divided the people of Assisi from those of Perugia). The Lord has glorified you above all your neighbors: you should therefore be very grateful to your Creator and humble yourself not only before the Almighty but even before your neighbors. And yet your heart is puffed up with arrogance, audacity, and pride. You pillage your neighbors and kill many of them. I also say to you, if you do not mend your ways very soon and if you do not make reparation for the damage you have caused, the Lord, who does not allow any injustice to be done without chastisement, is preparing a terrible vengeance, punishment, and humiliation for you. He will set you one against the other; discord and civil war will break out, and they will cause you worse calamities than those that could come to you from your neighbors."

[LP 35]

Neither the knights nor the citizens of Perugia heeded Francis' preaching. A few days after that famous sermon, feuding broke out among them. The civil war within Perugia caused much damage that could have been prevented if they had paid attention to the holy man from Assisi.

Innocent III died in Perugia on July 16, 1216. He was a very powerful pope and the historians of Perugia boast over the fact that he honored their city by dying there. Perhaps to offset their pride, a story emerged from a certain Cistercian Abbot who was living near Perugia in 1216. The Abbot declared he had a dream in which the eyes of his mind were opened. He saw a naked man with a papal mitre chased by a terrifying dragon, all the while shouting, "Have mercy on me, oh Thou most merciful God." When the Abbot awoke, he entered Perugia to receive the announcement that the Pope had died. The Abbot understood that he had seen Innocent III in his dream and he marveled at the mercy of Almighty God who treats the humble and the powerful with equal law and mercy. Innocent III's remains were buried at the Cathedral until Leo XIII transferred them to a specially prepared monument in Rome at the Basilica of St. John Lateran.

Today, when we arrive by public transportation at Perugia, we proceed on foot to stairways leading up through the Paolina Fortress to the center of the city. The fortress takes its name from Pope Paul III whose personal power brought about the merger of Perugia with the Papal States. Climbing up the steps to the uppermost level, we come out onto the city streets through the Government Building. The Corso Vannucci, a favorite street for "una passagiata" [the Italian pastime of taking a walk], stretches from this point to its northern end at the Great Fountain in the Piazza IV Novembre. The fountain--referred to as the "apple of

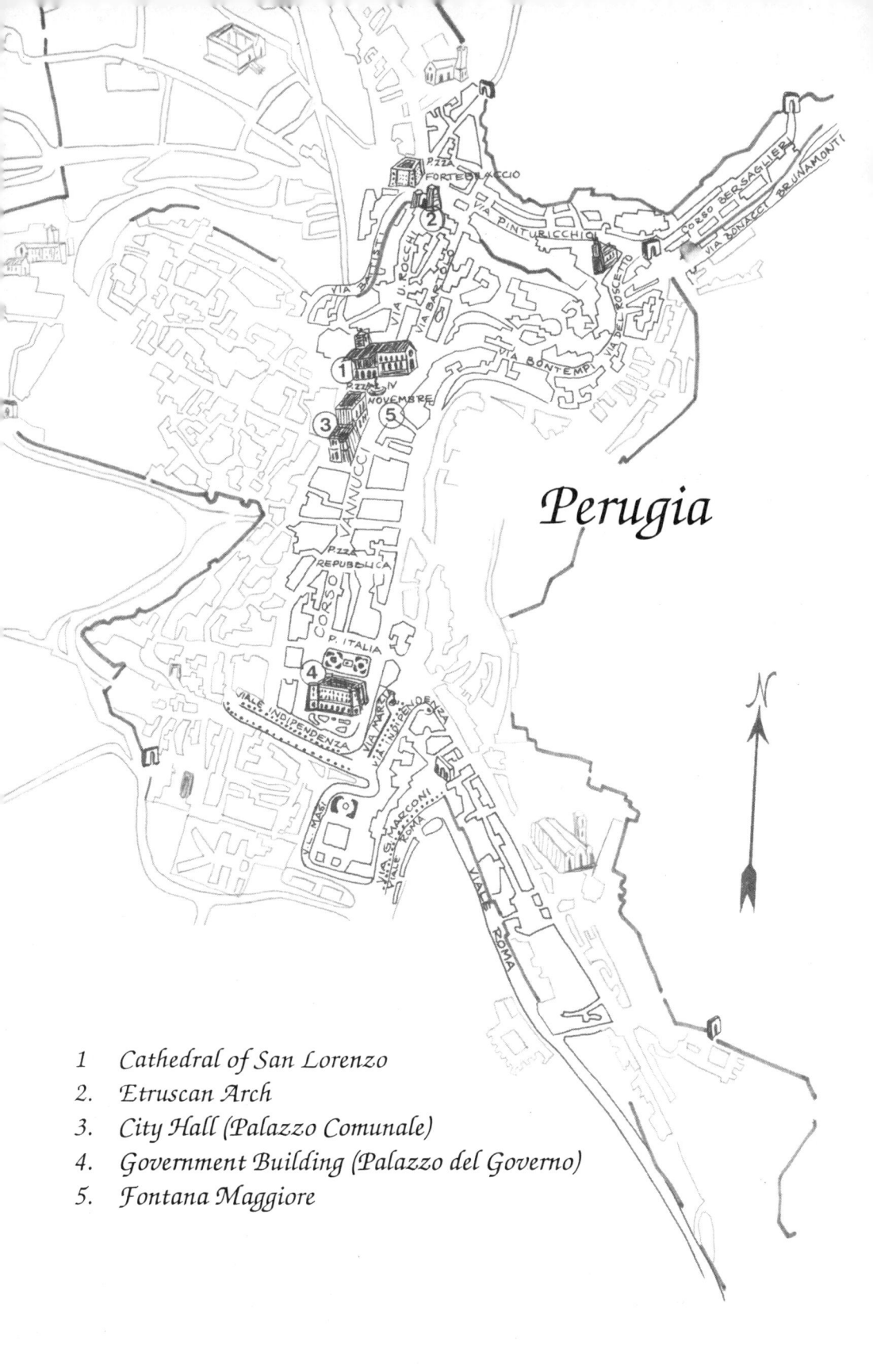

Perugia

1. Cathedral of San Lorenzo
2. Etruscan Arch
3. City Hall (Palazzo Comunale)
4. Government Building (Palazzo del Governo)
5. Fontana Maggiore

the eye of Perugia"—was designed by Friar Bevignate around 1277 A.D. At the fountain we view the lateral facade of the Cathedral of San Lorenzo, the entrance to the bishop's palace (Canonica) and, to the south, the City Hall which is also referred to as the Palazzo Comunale, or Priori Palace.

Further Reflection

Consider the feelings that Mary, the mother of Jesus, experienced when she heard Him reply, "Who is my mother?" "Whoever does the will of my heavenly Father is my brother, and sister, and mother" (Mt.12:50). Then, consider Ortulana's role as mother of three daughters who left home because they "took a spouse of a more noble lineage"(1LAg 7). Ortulana taught her daughters the basics of the Christian life while they were in exile, but could she have imagined where their love for Jesus would lead them? She observed a new spiritual maturation blossoming forth in her own offspring. Did she struggle with a spirit of possessiveness of her beautiful daughters? Or did she encourage them to "leave mother and father" and "take nothing for the journey" in order to follow in the footsteps of Christ?

When Jesus told the crowds that anyone who did the will of His Father was thereby His brother and mother and sister, He described the manner in which persons would become members of the heavenly assembly, the "cloud of witnesses." The Letter to the Hebrews offers encouragement to all who aspire to join such a family:

Therefore, since we are surrounded by so great a cloud of witnesses, let us rid ourselves of every burden and sin that clings to us and persevere in running the race that lies before us while keeping our eyes fixed on Jesus, the leader and perfecter of faith. For the sake of the joy that lay before him he endured the cross, despising its shame, and has taken his seat at the right of the throne of God.   [Heb 12: 1-2]

How might we learn from Ortulana to step back in order for others to deepen their intimacy with God ?

Suggested Readings

Bartoli, Marco. *Clare of Assisi*. Trans. Sr. Frances Marie. Quincy, IL: The Franciscan Press, 1993.

Portiuncula

The Portiuncula

Clare at the Portiuncula

Strength of faith, energy of conviction, and counsel from Francis were the inspirations guiding Clare as she wound her way toward the Portiuncula in the darkness of the Palm Sunday night in March of 1212. She ran after Christ without being burdened or restrained by anything, as the *Legend* notes:

> And so she ran to Saint Mary of the Portiuncula, leaving behind her home, city, and relatives. There the brothers, who were observing sacred vigils before the little altar of God, received the virgin Clare with torches. There, immediately after rejecting the filth of Babylon, she gave the world "a bill of divorce." There, her hair shorn by the hands of the brothers, she put aside every kind of fine dress.
>
> Was it not fitting
> that an Order of flowering virginity
> be awakened
> in the evening
> or in any other place
> than in this place of her,
> the first and most worthy of all,
> who alone is Mother and Virgin!
>
> [LegCL, 8]

Investiture of Clare

Clare's investiture became known throughout the Umbrian Valley. The witness of Lord Ugolino de Pietro Giradone, a knight of Assisi, confirms the public knowledge of the event:

> Asked how he knew the virgin of God, Clare, had entered Religion through the preaching of Saint Francis, he replied this was public knowledge and known by everyone. He had heard Saint Francis gave her the tonsure in the church of Saint Mary of the Portiuncula. After she had entered the monastery of San Damiano, he had heard and noticed--it was obvious--that she was of such holiness and goodness in her Order she might be like any other saint in heaven. [Proc XVI,6]

Clare's sister, Beatrice, testified that Clare had received the tonsure:

> Saint Francis gave her the tonsure before the altar in the church of the Virgin Mary, called the Portiuncula. [Proc XII,4]

For forty-one years after her consecration, Clare viewed the Portiuncula out in the valley amidst a few trees from her vantage point at San Damiano. The memory of the small sacred space served as a touchstone for meditation on the poverty of Mary, the "Virgin made Church." Clare valued and praised the poverty of "so great and good a Lord...coming into the Virgin's womb (1LAg 19)." Her meditation on the physical poverty of the Lord sustained her in her choice for a life of austerity. Toward the end of her life she recalled the reputation she and the Sisters had:

When the blessed Francis saw, however, that, although we were physically weak and frail, we did not shirk deprivation, poverty, hard work, trial, or the shame or contempt of the world--rather, we considered them as delights, as he had frequently examined us according to the example of the saints and his brothers--he greatly rejoiced in the Lord. And moved by compassion for us, he bound himself, both through himself and through his Order, to always have the same loving care and special solicitude for us as for his own brothers... Afterwards he wrote a form of life for us, especially that we always persevere in holy poverty. While he was living he was not content to encourage us with many words and examples to the love of holy poverty and its observance, but he gave us many writings that, after his death, we would in no way turn away from it, as the Son of God never wished to abandon this holy poverty while He lived in the world. [TestC 27-29, 33-36]

A story of questionable authority attempts to highlight the Portiuncula by situating Francis and Clare meeting there. According to the *Little Flowers of St. Francis* which dates from the fifteenth century, Francis' companions had pleaded with him to have greater compassion on Clare by permitting her to have a meal with him. Francis replied:

> I agree. But in order to give her greater pleasure, I want this meal to be at St. Mary of the Angels, for she has been cloistered at San Damiano for a long time and she

> will enjoy seeing once more for a while the Place of St. Mary where she was shorn and made a spouse of the Lord Jesus Christ. So we will eat there together, in the name of the Lord. [Fior, no. 15]]

When the day arrived and they were grouped around a humble table, Francis and Clare began to converse in such a sweet and profound manner that all present were enraptured with the Divine Presence. To the folks in the valley it appeared that the place of the Portiuncula was on fire and so they came running with water buckets only to discover the saints and their companions seated in conversation around their simple table. When Francis and Clare came back to themselves, they felt so spiritually nourished that they had no appetite for additional food. Clare left the blessed meal to return to her monastery with the Poor Ladies.

Historical Background

In the months following his conversion, Saint Francis lived the life of a penitent and spent his energies repairing three churches. After finishing the church of St. Peter, situated in the valley far from Assisi, he came to the place called the Portiuncula. Bonaventure describes the role that this small poor church had in Francis' life:

> He came to a place called the Portiuncula where there was an old church dedicated to the Virgin Mother of God which was now abandoned with no one to look after it. Francis had great devotion to the Queen of the world

and when he saw that the church was deserted, he began to live there constantly in order to repair it. He heard that the angels often visited it, so that it used to be called St. Mary of the Angels, and he decided to stay there permanently out of reverence for the angels and love for the Mother of Christ. He loved this spot more than any other in the world. It was here that he began his religious life in a very small way; it was here that he made such extraordinary progress, and it was here that he came to a happy end. When he was dying, he commended this spot above all others to the friars, because it was most dear to the Blessed Virgin.

[LM II, 8]

Francis' zeal for rebuilding churches was known by the young Clare who expressed her desire to be a partner to this project by contributing money. The modesty and humility of Clare's penitential lifestyle restrained her from public affairs so she sent Lady Bona to deliver the donation. Lady Bona herself testified:

> Lady Clare, while she was still in the world, also gave the witness a certain amount of money as a votive offering and directed her to carry it to those who were working on Saint Mary of the Portiuncula so that they would sustain the flesh. [Proc XVII, 7]

Francis was attending Mass in the small chapel on February 24, 1208, when he heard the Gospel proclaimed that touched his heart and emerged into his consciousness as the meaning for his life. What he heard was the Lord's message to the disciples: "Carry no purse, no bag, no sandals; and greet no one on the road. Whatever house you enter, first say, 'Peace to this house!' (Luke 10:4-5)." Celano describes Francis' response:

> [Francis] immediately cried out exultingly: "This is what I wish, this is what I seek, this is what I long to do with all my heart." Then the holy father, **overflowing with joy**, hastened to fulfill that salutary word he had heard, and he did not suffer any delay to intervene before beginning devoutly to perform what he had heard. He immediately put off his shoes from his feet, put aside the staff from his hands, was content with one tunic, and exchanged his leather girdle for a small cord. He designed for himself a tunic that bore a likeness to the cross, that by means of it he might beat off all temptations of the devil; he designed a very rough tunic so that by it he might crucify the flesh with all its vices and sins; he designed a very poor and mean tunic, one that would not excite the covetousness of the world. The other things that he had heard, however, he longed with the greatest diligence and the greatest reverence to perform. For he was not a deaf hearer of the Gospel, but committing all that he had heard to praiseworthy memory, he tried diligently to carry it out to the letter.
>
> [1Cel 22]

Later, when he had companions, Francis faced the responsibility of providing a place where the friars might pray the Hours—and also a place for burial of their deceased—by begging for such a place.

> So he went to the Bishop of Assisi and put this request to him. But the Bishop said, "Brother, I have no church to offer you," and the Canons gave the same answer. Then he went to the Abbot of S. Benedict on Monte Subasio, and made the same request to him. The Abbot was roused to sympathy, and took counsel with his monks; and guided by the grace and will of God, he granted to blessed Francis and his friars the church of St. Mary of the Portiuncula, which was the smallest and poorest church they had. And the Abbot said to blessed Francis, "See, Brother, we have granted your request. But if the Lord causes this congregation of yours to grow, we wish this place to become the chief of all your churches." His suggestion pleased blessed Francis and his brethren, and he was delighted with this place granted to the friars, especially since the church was named after the Mother of Christ, and was so poor and small.
>
> [SpPer 55]

Thus it came about that Francis and his first brothers received the Portiuncula as the chief of all their churches. Here they held their chapters and here the investiture of Clare took place on Palm Sunday evening, 1212.

Today, we enter the grand Basilica of St. Mary of the Angels in order to approach the sacred chapel of the Portiuncula.

The small chapel rebuilt by Francis became a major pilgrimage site after, according to the legend, he received a divine inspiration that was later confirmed by Pope Honorius in 1216: those who with sincere and contrite hearts would cross the threshold into the Portiuncula to pray would receive pardon from all their past sins and be assured of their salvation. At first this "Il Perdono" [the Pardon] could be received only on August 2, the anniversary of the day the announcement was made, because of the consternation of bishops of other major pilgrimage sites who thought the ease of obtaining the Pardon would discourage pilgrimages to their own shrines.

In 1927, the Pardon became accessible at the Portiuncula every day of the year. Pilgrims may receive a plenary indulgence by being free from attachment to sin, receiving the sacraments of penance and the Eucharist, visiting the church and praying especially for the intentions of the pope. Since 1967, the plenary indulgence of the Portiuncula may be obtained in every church in the world, reflecting our current emphasis that salvation is achieved through virtuous living more than seeking indulgences.

A painting from 1392 that hangs above the altar in the small chapel depicts the legend of the Portiuncula Indulgence. The episodes are to be viewed counterclockwise from the lower right: 1) Francis praying near his cell receives mercy from Our Lord Jesus Christ. A fleeing devil depicts the power of prayer conquering sinful desires. 2) Francis exchanges all earthly riches for Lady Poverty, depicted by Francis throwing himself into thorn bushes for mortification. Francis experiences assurance of his salvation and desires the same for others. He gathers a bouquet of roses to carry

"Il Perdono"

to the heavenly throne. 3) Choirs of angels surround Mary and Jesus who convey to Francis the gift of the "Il Perdono" [the Pardon]--all repentant persons could receive mercy and pardon by crossing the threshold of the Portiuncula. 4) Pope Honorius cannot refuse the humble Francis pleading for the "Il Perdono" when the saint says that Jesus Christ has sent him for this request. 5) Francis proclaims the new indulgence from a platform built in front of the Portiuncula--the bishops of the Umbrian valley look on while the laity hear the Good News. 6) Mary's posture in the Annunciation picture reveals her timidity and humility as the angel Gabriel comes as a messenger from God.

Pope Pius V decreed the construction of the Basilica of St. Mary of the Angels in 1569. The Dominican pope had a great love for the Blessed Virgin which both motivated him to have a large basilica built in her honor and, at the same time, to accommodate the huge crowds of pilgrims who arrived there for the August 2nd Feast of the Pardon. In 1832 an earthquake devastated the basilica except for the pillars and dome protecting the sacred Portiuncula chapel. The main portion of the basilica was rebuilt soon afterwards, 1836-40. The provinces of Friars Minor in the United States donated the funds for the reconstruction of the facade of the basilica for the seventh centenary of the death of Francis. In the course of some excavations in the crypt beneath the high altar, during 1966-70, new discoveries were made of the foundation for the first friary erected on the site by the townspeople for the friars.

Pope John Paul II celebrated an Ecumenical World Day of Peace at the Portiuncula with world religious leaders on October 26, 1986. The impact of this event of unity in prayer continues to

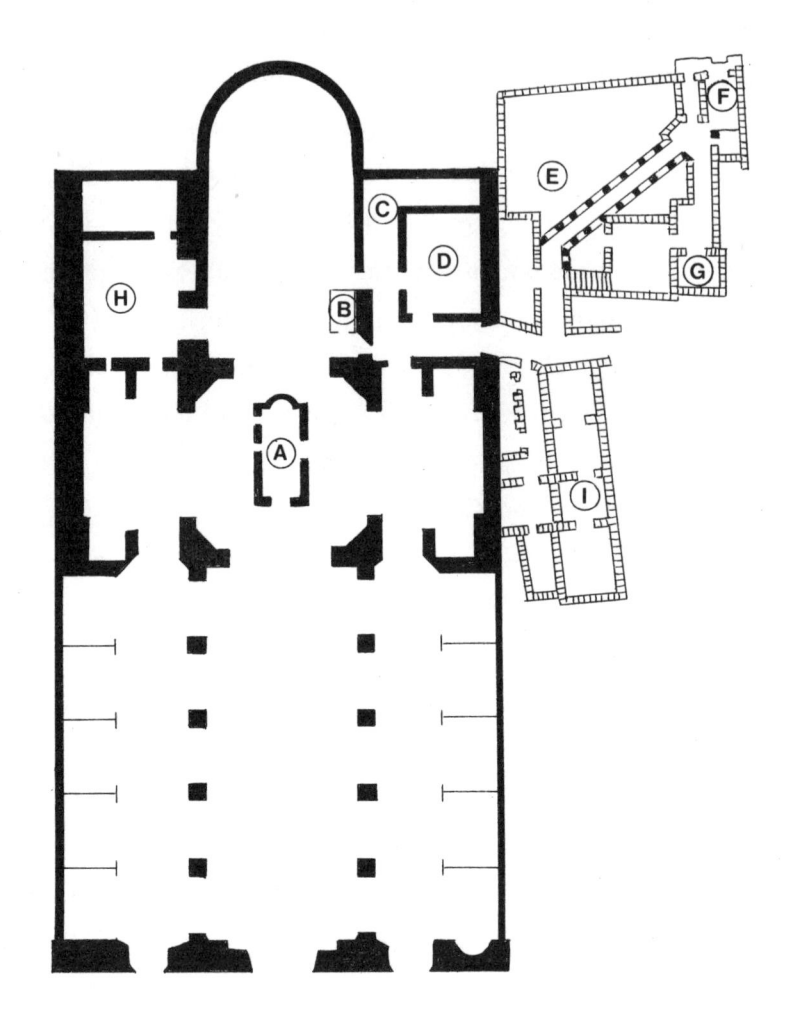

Basilica of S. Mary of the Angels

A. Portiuncula
B. Transitus Chapel
C. Entrance to Crypt
D. Sacristy
E. Rose Garden
F. Chapel of the Roses
G. Chapel of the Weeping Francis
H. Blessed Sacrament Chapel
I. Museum

offer hope and inspiration to others. On October 23, 1992, Pope John Paul II held a private audience with the fresco artist, Mark Balma, and his wife, Louise, along with a 43-member commission promoting "Frescoes for Assisi." The pontiff blessed the committee promoting the art project which will cover the entire ceiling vaults of the Basilica of St. Mary of the Angels with an art legacy of pictures depicting reconciliation. Cycles of frescoes portraying accounts of reconciliation from the Hebrew Scriptures, the New Testament and the life of Francis will continue to speak to pilgrims for generations to come of the invitation to all races and creeds to become peacemakers so that the human family may be reconciled to each other and the Creator from whom all blessings flow.

Further Reflection

The Spirit of the Lord leads us into the unimaginable depths of intimacy within the Trinitarian life. The activity of the Spirit at work in Francis and Clare while they prayed at the Portiuncula transformed them into co-workers with Jesus in union with the Spirit manifesting new expressions of divine love. The Portiuncula is the womb of the Franciscan movement:

> This is the place in which a new army of the poor, under the leadership of Francis, took its joyful beginnings, so that it might be clearly seen that it was the Mother of mercies who brought to birth both Orders in her dwelling place.   [LegCl 8]

Clare presents to the Franciscan imagination a supreme paradox of expression of poverty. She developed her understanding of poverty through devotion to the virgin from Nazareth from whom the world came to know Jesus: out of littleness comes greatness, out of poverty comes richness, out of virginity comes motherhood. Clare's own writings open the window to her experience of poverty:

> O blessed poverty, who bestows eternal riches on those who love and embrace her!

> O holy poverty, God promises the kingdom of heaven and, in fact, offers eternal glory and a blessed life to those who possess and desire you!

> O God-centered poverty, whom the Lord Jesus Christ, Who ruled and now rules heaven and earth, Who spoke and things were made, condescended to embrace before all else!

> The foxes have dens, He says, and the birds of the air have nests, but the Son of Man, Christ, has nowhere to lay His head, but bowing His head gave up His spirit. If so great and good a Lord, then, on coming into the Virgin's womb, chose to appear despised, needy, and poor in this world so that people who were in utter poverty, want and absolute need of heavenly nourishment might become rich in Him by possessing

the kingdom of heaven, be very joyful and glad! Be filled with a remarkable happiness and a spiritual joy! Because, since contempt of the world has pleased You more than its honors, poverty more than earthly riches, and You have sought to store up greater treasures in heaven rather than on earth, where rust does not consume nor moth destroy nor thieves break in and steal, your reward is very rich in heaven!

[1LAg 15-24]

Today, what form of poverty makes our lives rich and fruitful?

Suggested Reading

Doino, Joseph. "Francis and Mary Revisited." *Cord* 37(1987):141-43.

Fortini, Arnaldo. *Francis of Assisi.* Trans. Helen Moak. New York: Crossroad, 1981. 381-385.

Iriarte, Lazaro. "Clare of Assisi: Her Place in Female Hagiography." *Greyfriars Review* 3/2 (1989): 173-206.

Macquarrie, John. *Mary For All Christians.* Grand Rapids, MI: William B. Eerdmans, 1991.

If you die with Him on the cross of tribulation, you shall possess heavenly mansions in the splendor of the saints

Monastery of San Paolo

Clare at San Paolo

Following the ceremony of investiture at the Portiuncula, Francis directed Clare to go to a Benedictine monastery called San Paolo delle Abbadesse [Saint Paul of the Abbesses]. There she found refuge at the altar in the chapel when her angry uncle, Monaldo, and some other knights attempted, but failed, to bring her back home:

> But after the news reached her relatives, they condemned with a broken heart the deed and proposal of the virgin and, banding together as one, they ran to the place, attempting to obtain what they could not. They employed violent force, poisonous advice, and flattering promises, trying to persuade her to give up such a worthless deed that was unbecoming to her class and without precedence in her family. But, taking hold of the altar cloths, she bared her tonsured head, maintaining that she would in no way be torn away from the service of Christ. With the increasing violence of her relatives, her spirit grew and her love--provoked by injuries--provided strength. So, for many days, even

> though she endured an obstacle in the way of the Lord and her own relatives opposed her proposal of holiness, her spirit did not crumble and her fervor did not diminish. Instead, amid words and deeds of hatred, she molded her spirit anew in hope until her relatives, turning back, were quiet. [LegCl 9]

Clare's first days in religious life were lived with the Benedictines during the liturgical highlight of the year, Holy Week. Those days at the monastery bore great fruit in Clare's life. First of all, Clare benefited from her knowledge and experience of life in a Benedictine monastery. Later on in her life, she wove together the church's desire that she live the Benedictine Rule with her desire to be an abbess of a community of Poor Ladies who lived the form of life given them from Francis. Secondly, Clare's experience of her relatives' rejection and violence encouraged her to identify more closely with the experience of Christ's sufferings which were liturgically celebrated that Holy Week at San Paolo.

Clare's brief stay at San Paolo provided her with some experiential knowledge of monasticism and assisted her to clarify her choices as a leader for a new form of religious life. We might understand this clarification of choices in terms of "discernment." Clare was led by the Spirit through stages of spiritual development. Her reflection upon her time in the Benedictine monastery bore fruit in further clarity of the choices that the Spirit invited her to make for her authentic response to her own inner call. Clare's leadership in establishing a new expression of

Gospel living for women can be better understood and appreciated by a study of her relation to thirteenth century spirituality. San Paolo provided Clare with observation of the women's monastic holdings of great financial security. She would have observed, and perhaps experienced, the power of authority held by the abbess. The Benedictine communal prayer life consisted mainly in the chanting of the Liturgy of the Hours which required choral training. Clare's life reflects her contrasting values of poverty, shared authority within the community and a simpler communal prayer form.

The second aspect of Clare's life that remained constant after San Paolo was her love of the Crucified Christ. Her own rejection and abuse suffered from her relatives more quickly united her with Jesus on the Cross. She once told Brother Raynaldo:

> After I once came to know the grace of my Lord Jesus Christ through his servant Francis, no pain has been bothersome, no penance too severe, no weakness, dearly beloved brother, has been hard. [LegCl 44]

One particular Good Friday, much later in her life, Clare was completely absorbed in the exchange of love with Our Lord on the cross. Sister Filippa recalled that day;

> Lady Clare was so caught up in her contemplation that during the day of Good Friday, while thinking about the Passion of the Lord, she was almost insensible throughout that entire day and a large part of the following day. [Proc III,25]

She taught her companions to be ever grateful for the love poured out by Jesus on the Cross. When Easter arrived, after celebrating the Lord's Resurrection and distributing the blessed Easter water, Clare exhorted her sisters:

> My sisters and daughters, you must always remember and recall this blessed water that came from the right side of our Lord Jesus Christ as He hung upon the cross.
>
> [Proc XIV, 8]

Her attachment to the Crucified is revealed in her writing addressed to Agnes in Prague:

> If you suffer with Him, you will reign with Him. [If you] weep [with Him], you shall rejoice with Him; [If you] die with Him on the cross of tribulation, you shall possess heavenly mansions in the splendor of the saints .
>
> [2LAg 21]

After that memorable Holy Week at the Benedictine monastery, Clare left there to join another community of women at Sant'Angelo in Panzo on the slope of Mount Subasio.

Historical Background

The monastic community of San Paolo delle Abbadesse [Saint Paul of the Abbesses] was situated near the small city of Bastia. Bastia quietly rests along the Chiascio river west of Assisi about four kilometers. All of this region was a lake in pre-historic times but gradually the waters recessed. During the Roman era, a town was built on a rise in the midst of a vast expanse of stagnant waters; this town was referred to as *Insula Romana* and later called Bastia. The water level of the region dropped suddenly about four meters in 1400 when the Chiascio river, which drains the floor of the Umbrian valley, burst through some rocky dikes carrying stagnant waters out of the valley.

San Paolo was well known for its affluence; this was probably due to the dowries given by the noble families when they presented a daughter to the monastery. Innocent III identified this monastery in 1198 as one of the women's communities under the jurisdiction of Bishop Guido of Assisi. Francis and Clare would have known of a papal privilege of sanctuary granted in 1201 to this monastery; the privilege provided a safe haven for Clare since excommunication was imposed upon anyone who would perform an act of violence at the monastery. At the end of the 13th century, the monastery community moved into a new house in Assisi near the bishop's residence. In 1452, this monastery was united with that of the monastery of Sant'Apollinare.

Today, the romanesque chapel of San Paolo delle Abbadesse monastery, which harbored Clare during the Holy Week following her investiture at the Portiuncula, serves as a mortuary chapel for Bastia's cemetery. Plaques on the interior walls of the chapel remind us of Clare's history at this place and, at the same time, demonstrate the longstanding cult of Clare maintained by the local townspeople. To drive to the cemetery from Assisi, take the road leading west beneath the hill on which stands St. Francis basilica. Immediately, drive across the bridge over the dry Tescio River and watch on the right side for the tall cypress trees standing erect around the cemetery. The cemetery wall blocks the view of chapels that are within the area: one rather modern one has an aluminum cross that stands high above others. The San Paolo chapel is the one with the portal facing the west and the river. Here we may enter and remember Clare's conviction to follow in the footsteps of Our Lord Jesus Christ, not; a conviction that was tested and confirmed in this chapel.

Further Reflection

Clare's devotion to the humanity of Christ expresses a significant commonality with Francis. Ortulana was the first to instill in Clare a love for Jesus; her motherly affection and faith imbued her vivid descriptive accounts of her own pilgrimage experiences to the Holy Land, the sacred places of Jesus' life and death. It was Francis who taught Clare to further love the Cross by teaching her his own Office of the Passion:

> She learned the Office of the Cross as Francis, a lover of the Cross, had established it and recited it with similar affection. Underneath her habit she girded her flesh with a small cord marked with thirteen knots, a secret reminder of the wounds of the Savior.   [LegCl 30]

When Clare was dying, she begged the sisters to remain in prayer. They remembered how she had frequently repeated the Prayer of the Five Wounds of the Lord, so one of the Sisters prayed that familiar prayer aloud for Clare to hear.

The witness [Sister Agnes] said the Prayer of the Five Wounds of the Lord. As if Lady Clare were able to understand, but speaking very softly, she continually kept the Passion of the Lord on her lips and so the name of the Lord Jesus Christ. [Proc X, 10]

What prayer is my entryway into the heart of Jesus Crucified?

Suggested Readings

De Robeck, Nesta. *St. Clare of Assisi*. Chicago: Franciscan Herald Press, 1951,1980.

De Sainte-Marie, Henri. "Presence of the Benedictine Rule in the Rule of St. Clare." *Greyfriars Review* 6/1 (1992): 49 - 66.

Sant'Angelo in Panzo

Sant' Angelo in Panzo

Clare at Sant'Angelo

When Clare left the Benedictine monastery after a few days, she was accompanied by Francis, Phillip and Bernard on her walk from San Paolo near Bastia to Sant'Angelo in Panzo on the hillside of Mount Subasio. This journey on foot took place Easter Sunday or the beginning of Easter Week. The Gospel account of Jesus walking with the disciples on the road to Emmaus embodies the sacramentality of the moment. Were not the hearts of those four early Franciscans burning within them as they walked up to Mount Subasio! They were turning their backs on a secure monastic institutional setting as they faced the insecurity of lives of voluntary poverty.

At Sant'Angelo, Clare joined a community of penitential women. There Agnes, her sister, joined her. The departure of two women from the Offreduccio household embarrassed the knights who felt obliged to protect the young women from foolishly leaving the opportunities for marriage, wealth and worldly gain. The self-determination of Clare and Agnes provoked the ire of the men and led to violence as recorded in Clare's Legend:

For while the joyous sisters were clinging to the footprints of Christ in the church of San Angelo in Panzo and she who had heard more from the Lord was teaching her novice-sister, new attacks by relatives were quickly flaring up against the young girls. The next day, hearing that Agnes had gone off to Clare, twelve men, burning with anger and hiding outwardly their evil intent, ran to the place [and] pretended [to make] a peaceful entrance. Immediately they turned to Agnes--since they had long ago lost hope of Clare--and said: "Why have you come to this place? Get ready to return immediately with us!" When she responded that she did not want to leave her sister Clare, one of the knights in a fierce mood ran toward her and, without sparing blows and kicks, tried to drag her away by her hair, while the others pushed her and lifted her in their arms. At this, as if she had been captured by lions and been torn from the hands of the Lord, the young girl cried out: "Dear sister, help me! Do not let me be taken from Christ the Lord!" While the violent robbers were dragging the young girl along the slope of the mountain, ripping her clothes and strewing the path with the hair [they had] torn out, Clare prostrated herself in prayer with tears, begged that her sister would be given constancy of mind and that the strength of humans would be overcome by divine power.

[LegCl 25]

Clare's prayer was heard; the knights were unable to carry Agnes because her body had become so heavy she was immovable. After the noblemen left the scene, Agnes got up rejoicing with great resolve to commit her life to the Lord. There in the chapel of Sant'Angelo in Panzo, Francis received Agnes into religious life and gave her the grey habit of penance and the tonsure.

The third daughter of Favarone and Ortulana, Beatrice, was still at home when Agnes left. She recounted that Clare and Agnes remained at Sant'Angelo for a short time before they began the monastery at San Damiano;

> Saint Francis, Brother Filippo and Brother Bernard took her to the church of Sant'Angelo di Panzo, where she stayed for a little time, and then to the church of San Damiano where the Lord gave her more sisters for her direction. [Proc XII,5]

Why did Clare leave Sant'Angelo? It was apparently a small community and in a geographically isolated place outside of the city. The evidence that she was not satisfied to be a member of this Beguine-type community was told by her hagiographer:

> After a few days, she went to the church of San Angelo in Panzo, where her mind was not completely at peace, so that, at the advice of Saint Francis, she moved to San Damiano. [LegCl 10]

Historical Background

The hillside east of Assisi attracted Romans desiring to construct dwelling places because it had 1) spring water and 2) the location provided a scenic and comfortable reception of the midday sun with cooling breezes from the mountain. The name "Panzo" is believed to be the surname of the family that built an ancient villa here, complete with its own chapel. The chapel's name is a derivative of St. Michael Archangel, reflecting a cult popular with the people. In 1333, the diocese of Assisi listed thirteen churches named after this archangel. Sant'Angelo is one of them.

By the time Innocent III became pope, the penitential movement was widespread, including communities of women living together in their own homes. This great pope wanted to reform the church and restore social order in a chaotic society. What was he to do with those groups of women who were not living according to any Rule of religious life, nor any subjection to a feudal lord? In 1198, he wrote to Bishop Guido in Assisi and declared that all such groups in the Assisi diocese in the Umbrian valley would come under obedience to the bishop. The women at Sant'Angelo were a community that could be classified as a version of the Italian Beguines, sometimes referred to as *bizzoche*. They had no formal religious rule and became subject to Bishop Guido. Therefore, when Francis led Clare to this monastery for women at Sant'Angelo in Panzo, he took her to a community of penitents whose place of residence at their privately-owned property had come under the jurisdiction of the diocese.

Records show that by 1238 the women at Sant'Angelo in Panzo chose to develop their form of life as "Damianites," that is patterned after the Poor Ladies at San Damiano. After Clare died, Assisians were quite concerned about the welfare of these women outside the city walls. Sant'Angelo's community moved into the city in 1270, leaving their residence abandoned. It was not until the 15th century that the ruins were renovated to their original purpose, a private home.

Today, Sant'Angelo remains a private villa. In 1604, Duke Ferrante Bonacquisti reconstructed the little church that harbored Clare and Agnes during their first weeks of religious life. In 1933 it became the property of the Brunelli family; a descendant, Dr. Ettore Marconi, is the present owner.

Further Reflection

What was Clare seeking? Perhaps the community of women was too financially secure to offer Clare a place where she could keep company with Lady Poverty. Fortini states that "the very air was heavy with a dull prosperity, and in it there was no room for mystic rushes of renunciation." The friendship of Francis and Clare was based on doing what was holy and pleasing to the Lord. Clare's calling to live evangelical life with women in community was given impetus by the witness of Francis and his early companions. The absolute poverty that Francis and the friars embraced was their response to the Gospel. They imagined how Jesus and his disciples went out two by two without any money, any staff and no extra clothes, and they desired with all their hearts to do likewise. The literal interpretation of the Gospel, inflamed by the love of the Holy Spirit at work within these saints, gave them the "rule and life" to guide the totality of their lives. Their criteria for discernment was their desire to follow in the footsteps of Our Lord Jesus Christ.

Clare's restlessness at Sant'Angelo indicates a stage of her conversion to a deeper surrender to God. Like Mary, the Virgin-Mother, Clare received a call and recognized that the Spirit of the Lord would lead her. She needed a sign from God that she was to live a community life with women in a similar manner as Francis and his companions--poor and dependent on alms. The unmistakable sign was divine intervention preventing Clare's sister, Agnes, from being hauled back home by their angry relatives. Agnes' unexplainable resistance to being dragged away is considered the result of Clare's prayerful intercession for her sister. This is identified as Clare's first miracle, after which Francis invested Agnes in the chapel at Sant'Angelo. These siblings formed the nucleus of the community of women whose lives became the fulfillment of the prophecy for San Damiano:

> For at that time, climbing the wall of that church, he shouted in French to some poor people who were standing nearby: "Come and help me in the work [of building] the monastery of San Damiano, because ladies will dwell here who will glorify our heavenly Father throughout His holy, universal Church by their celebrated and holy manner of life.   [TestC 13-14]

Perhaps it was Clare's premonition that she and Agnes were the fulfillment of the San Damiano prophecy that compelled her not to settle in at Sant'Angelo. Or are there other considerations in her discernment?

Clare was attracted to follow in the footsteps of Jesus according to the spirit of Francis: "Take nothing for your journey."

She had chosen freely and deliberately to be invested into religious life as one of the followers of Francis and his company of early companions. The ceremony at the Portiuncula needs to be remembered when reflecting on Clare's choice for her living situation. She demonstrated from the very beginning that she did not want to join other existing types of women's communities. Rather, she sought to live a new expression of radical poverty hitherto unknown for medieval women. Could it be that Clare's desire caused her to leave Sant'Angelo because the community there had the security of private ownership of property? It appears that she could not be satisfied until she had expressed a more complete abandonment to God in imitation of Our Lord Jesus Christ who hung naked on the cross in complete surrender to His Father. Clare desired to detach herself from everything that might keep her from "running and not tiring" (4LAg 31) in her pursuit of God's love.

What is it that we seek with all our heart?
What "security" inhibits our response to live the Gospel?

Suggested Reading

Fortini, A. *Francis of Assisi*. New York: Crossroad, 1981. 344-47.
Guarnieri, Romana. "Beguines Beyond the Alps and Italian Bizzoche between the 14th and 15th Centuries."*Greyfriars Review* 5/1 (1991): 93-104.
Miller, Ramona. "The Role of the Imagination in Franciscan Discernment." *Cord* 41/5 (1991): 131-40.
Santucci, Francesco. "S. Angelo di Panzo Presso Assisi." *ATTI: Accademia Properziana del Subasio - Assisi* Serie VI/13 (1986): 83-112.

San Damiano

San Damiano

Clare at San Damiano

After a few weeks at Sant'Angelo in Panzo, Clare and Agnes left to begin the simple way of life at San Damiano in austere poverty and rich simplicity. Their primary intention was to follow in the footsteps of Jesus in poverty and humility. In such a manner they sought to experience God and to possess everlasting life. Many years later, Clare described in a letter to Agnes of Prague her belief about entering into a life of prayer without possessions:

> What a great and praiseworthy exchange: to leave the things of time for those of eternity, to choose the things of heaven for the goods of earth, to receive the hundred-fold in place of one, and to possess a blessed eternal life!
>
> [1LAg 30]

The first fervor that motivated Clare to choose the contemplative life in poverty was sustained throughout her life. She lived at San Damiano for over forty years that form of life which she had received from Francis. Toward the end of her life, she incorporated Francis' directive into the Rule she composed:

> Since by divine inspiration you have made yourselves daughters and servants of the most high King, the heavenly Father, and have taken the Holy Spirit as your spouse, choosing to live according to the perfection of the Holy Gospel, I [Francis] resolve and promise for myself and for my brothers always to have that same loving care and special solicitude for you as [I have] for them.   [RCl VI,2]

Clare and her small community of Poor Ladies had been living at San Damiano about three years when Francis insisted Clare take the title of abbess. She did accept the title, but her style for government and direction of the Sisters broke from the traditional monastic norms. She placed herself in the role of servant to her Sisters:

> She never shirked any familial chores, to such an extent that she very often washed the hands of the sisters, assisted those who were seated [at table], and waited on those who were eating. Rarely would she give an order; instead she would do things spontaneously, preferring rather to do things herself than to order her sisters. She herself washed the mattresses of the sick; she herself, with that noble spirit of hers, cleansed them, not running away from their filth nor shrinking from their stench.
> [LegCl 12]

The essence of communal life at San Damiano was prayer. The ebb and flow of their prayer between private prayer and communal prayer was established around the Liturgy of the Hours. Sister Benvenuta describes the leadership of Clare for arising for Matins:

> Saint Clare was very assiduous, day and night, in prayer. At about midnight she woke the sisters with certain signs in silence to praise God. She lit the lamps in the church and frequently rang the bell for Matins. Those sisters who did not rise at the sound of the bell she called with her signs. [Proc II,9]

Sister Agnes testified that Clare would remain a very long time after Compline in "an abundance of tears" [Proc X,3]. Sister Angeluccia said that the same thing happened "in the morning at about the hour of Terce" [Proc XIV,2]. The passionate love that Clare had for her divine spouse moved her to prolonged periods of contemplation.

The enclosed life of the Poor Ladies preserved the necessary prayerful atmosphere sustaining the contemplative life. Lord Ugolino, a knight in Assisi whose testimony is contained in Clare's canonization process, called Clare the "first in the Order of Enclosed Ladies." From the experience and teaching of Clare, a form of religious life emerged that, according to her biographer, renewed the Church:

> Innumerable cities were enriched with monasteries, even fields and mountains were beautified with the structure of this celestial building. The cult of chastity intensified in

the world under the leadership of Clare and the renewed order of virgins was recalled in its midst. [LegCl 11]

Contemplative living requires a balance of work with the hands and time in private prayer. Clare's own example, as told by Sister Cecilia, taught the Sisters the importance of this balance:

> Lady Clare, never wanting to be idle at any time, even during the time of her last illness, made herself rise, sit up in bed and spin. The soft cloth made by her spinning she used to make many corporals and the cases to hold them, covered with silk or precious cloth. She sent them to the Bishop of Assisi, who blessed them, and then she sent them to the churches of the Assisi diocese. She believed they had been given to every church.
>
> [Proc VI,14]

The chronic illness of Clare that eventually forced her to be bedridden began about the same time as Francis' reception of the Stigmata. When she heard Francis was approaching his death, she wept bitterly because she desired to see him and feared she would die before Francis. According to Francis' companions,

> When Saint Francis pondered what she desired, that is, to see him, was impossible at that time since both of them were gravely ill, he wrote his blessing in a letter to comfort her and he also absolved her of all failings, if she had any, in obeying his commands and wishes and those of the Son of God. Moreover, that she might put away all grief and be consoled in the Lord, he told the brother

whom she had sent to him--yet the Spirit of God, not himself, spoke through him--"Go and take this letter to Lady Clare and tell her to put aside all sorrow and sadness because she cannot see me at this moment. But let her know that before she dies both she and her sisters will see me and have the greatest consolation from me."

[LP 109]

Clare lived for twenty-seven years after Francis' death, providing a stable presence to the fast growing Franciscan family. Her illness did not inhibit her from participating in the communal prayer life. If she was too ill to go down to the chapel, she could hear Mass in the upstairs oratory by opening the trap door above the altar.

When Clare's life was nearing the end, Sisters kept vigil in the dormitory. Some were around her weeping when they heard her speak to her soul. Sister Filippa recalled that Clare said,

"Go calmly in peace, for you will have a good escort, because He who created you has sent you the Holy Spirit and has always guarded you as a mother does her child who loves her." She added: "O Lord, may You who have created me, be blessed." [Proc III,20]

Some of the early companions of Francis came into the dormitory to read the Word of God to Clare and to bid fond farewell to their spiritual mother. According to the Legend,

When Brother Juniper appeared among them, that excellent jester of the Lord who uttered the Lord's words

> which were often warming, she was filled with a new joy and asked him if he had anything new from the Lord. When he opened his mouth he burst forth with words that were like burning sparks coming from the furnace of his fervent heart. The virgin of the Lord took great comfort in his parables. [LegCl 45]

Two other companions, Angelo and Leo, were there mourning along with the Sisters who were grieving the departure of Clare. Sister Benvenuta said she was thinking about the holiness of Clare and the heavenly welcome awaiting her when she saw this vision:

> She suddenly saw with her own eyes a great multitude of virgins, all dressed in white with crowns on their heads, coming and entering through the door of that room where the holy mother Clare was lying. Among these virgins there was one greater, above and beyond what could be described, far more beautiful than all the others, and wearing a crown upon her head larger than all the others. Above her crown she had a golden cluster in the form of a thurible from which such a brilliance came forth it seemed to illumine the entire house.
>
> These virgins approached the bed of holy Lady Clare. That virgin who seemed greater at first covered her bed with the most delicate cloth so fine that, even though she was covered with it, Lady Clare nonetheless saw through its great delicacy. Then the virgin of virgins, who was greater, inclined her face above the virgin Saint

> Clare, or above her breast, so that the witness could not discern one from the other. After this was done, they all disappeared. [Proc XI,4]

Clare died on August 11, 1253. Her penitential life led her into the place of everlasting joy where she eternally praises God with all the angels and saints.

Clare's enclosed life at San Damiano did not remain a secret. Many persons recounted her goodness and told of her miracles so that her story became well known. Every year on June 22, Assisi remembers Clare's effective prayer for the defense of their city. The story of the historic intercessory power of Clare's prayer comes from Sister Filippa:

> One day, when the enemy had advanced to destroy Assisi, certain Saracens scaled the walls of the monastery and went down into the enclosure. The Sisters were greatly afraid. But the most holy mother comforted all of them, looked down on the troops, and said, "Do not be afraid, because they will not be able to hurt us." After saying this, she turned to the help of her usual prayer. The strength of the prayer was such that the hostile Saracens departed as if driven away without doing any harm nor touching anyone in the house. [Proc III, 18b]

The Saracens were turned away, but contrary to the image of Clare holding up a monstrance, Sister Francesca's testimony describes Clare prostrate on the ground:

> ...when the Saracens entered the cloister of the said monastery, the Lady made them bring her to the entrance of the refectory and bring a small box where there was the Blessed Sacrament of the Body of Our Lord Jesus Christ. Throwing herself prostrate on the ground in prayer, she begged with tears, saying among other things: "Lord, look upon these servants of yours, because I cannot protect them." Then the witness heard a voice of wonderful sweetness: "I will always defend you!" The Lady then prayed for the city, saying: "Lord, please defend the city as well!" The same voice resounded and said: "The city will endure many dangers, but it will be defended." Then the Lady turned to the sisters and told them: "Do not be afraid, because I am a hostage for you so that you will not suffer any harm now nor any other time as long as you wish to obey God's commandments." Then the Saracens left in such a way that they did not do any harm or damage. [Proc IX,2]

Not only did the Saracens flee without harming the Poor Ladies, but within the year Clare averted another threat which came to the city of Assisi. Once again, Sister Filippa tells us:

> ...the greatly feared Vitalis d'Aversa had been sent by the emperor with a great army to assault Assisi. Since he had asserted he would not leave Assisi until he had taken it, Lady Clare was told in order to prevent this danger. After she had heard this, the Lady, confident of God's power, called all the sisters, had them bring some

ashes and covered her unveiled head with them. Then the Lady placed the ashes on the heads of all the sisters and commanded them to go to prayer so the Lord God would free the city. [Proc III,19]

That very night Vitalis and his army left the vicinity, and ever since then Assisians celebrate their gratitude for Clare.

Clare's life would be shrouded in mystery were it not for the documented witness reports gathered in preparation for her canonization. From the testimony gathered from those who knew her, her hagiographer described Clare's life at San Damiano:

> There, as if casting the anchor of her soul in a secure site, she no longer wavered due to further changes of place, nor did she hesitate because of its smallness, nor did she fear its isolation...
>
> In this little house of penance the virgin Clare enclosed herself for love of her heavenly Spouse. Here she imprisoned her body for as long as it would live, hiding it from the turmoil of the world. In the hollow of this wall, the silver-winged dove, building a nest, gave birth to a gathering of virgins of Christ, founded a holy monastery, and began the Order of the Poor Ladies.
>
> Here on a path of penance she trampled upon the earth of her members, sowed the seeds of perfect justice, and showed her footprints to her followers by her own manner of walking. In this confined retreat for forty-two years she broke open the alabaster jar of her body by the scourgings of her discipline so that the house of

the Church would be filled with the fragrance of her ointments.   [LegCl,10]

Historical Background

San Damiano belongs to the category of sacred space that connects our inner self with cosmic planes of communication. Its history pre-dates Roman civilization. In the early Middle Ages, the gravel path leading to San Damiano was flanked by funerary monuments believed to be remains from pre-Roman times. The earliest indication that San Damiano continues an ancient recognition as sacred space is a subterranean grotto, a humanly-made underground cave. The actual location is beneath the room affectionately referred to as Clare's refectory. If we were able to enter the enclosure today, we would discover a narrow set of steps made of smoothly-hewn rocks leading into the underground area that is approximately 8' wide and 12' long. The cold damp feeling of subterranean space prompts an examination of the walls; the porous rocky earth appears solid because moisture laden clay fills all the pores of the limestone. Standing at the bottom of the steps, we would face the focal point on the opposite wall, the apse. This curved indentation into the western wall is about 20 inches wide. It is not carved out to the floor; rather, the base of the indentation provides a seat for a presider of a cultic rite. The pre-Roman dating of this cave stems from the fact that after the Roman occupation of Assisi three centuries before Christ's coming, the Romans had established their cultic practices centered at the Temple of Minerva.

Christianity was introduced into Assisi by St. Felician, whose preaching so disturbed the Roman pontifices (those men charged with overseeing the citizens' obedience to the Roman state religion) that they demanded that he leave town; he died at Foligno where he is honored at their Cathedral. Tradition established that the site of the sermon he preached at his expulsion was on the outskirts of Assisi along the path heading down to San Damiano. Felician's sermon has a bearing on the origins of a Christian church at the San Damiano location:

> Remember to venerate and adore the cross that I place for you here, in memory of Jesus Christ our Lord. Prostrate yourselves here [near an ancient mausoleum between Assisi and San Damiano]. Here raise to him your prayers, in the morning, and at noon, and when evening falls. Praise him and offer him your heart.
>
> [*Francis of Assisi*, 214]

The first Christian church named after St. Damian was perhaps constructed during the Byzantine era, following the inclusion of the names of Cosmas and Damian in the canon of the Mass during the reign of Pope Felix V (526-30). According to oral tradition, the church originally was named Cosmas and Damian but became commonly referred to as "San Damiano." Marino Bigaroni, O.F.M., has done extensive research to discover the architectural nature of the church of San Damiano before Francis' reconstruction. His thesis is that the church of 1030 A.D., the date of the earliest documentation for a church at the site, had three bodies for

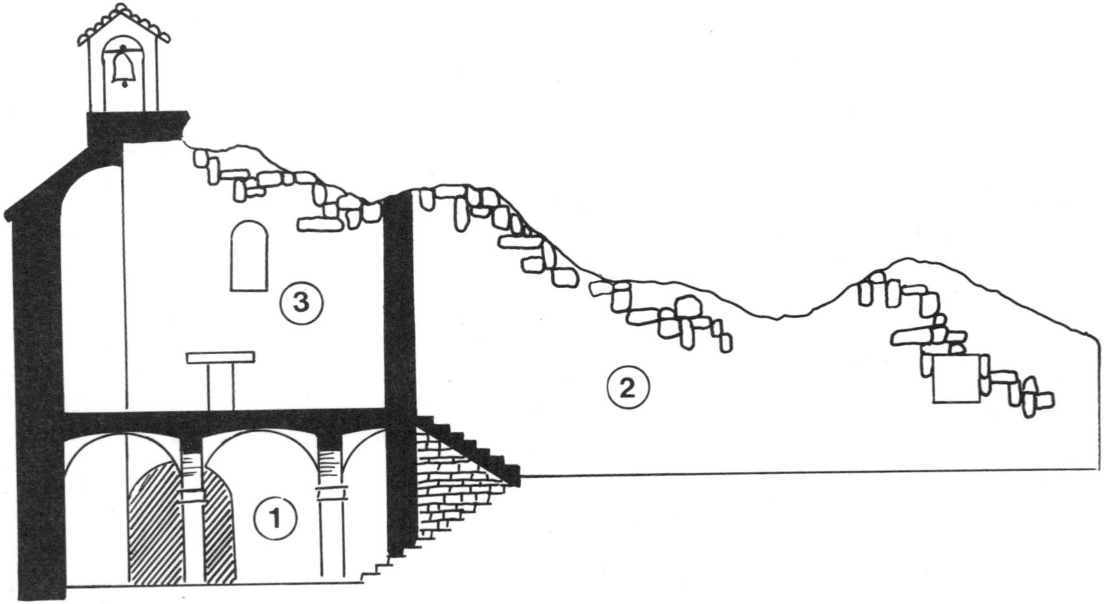

Ancient San Damiano

1. Crypt
2. Nave
3. Presbytery

liturgical space: the presbytery, crypt and nave, according to the design for a monastic foundation.

Francis had discovered the subterranean pre-Christian cave and found solace there as in a safe harbor in a storm. This secret place had not been altered at the time the Christians constructed their church parallel to the underground cave. The crypt of the Christian church was parallel to the cultic cave which was left undisturbed. The site matches Celano's detailed clue: "That pit was in that house and was known probably to one person alone."

> But he, the new athlete of Christ, when he heard of the threats of those who were pursuing him and when he got knowledge of their coming, wanting to give place to wrath, hid himself in a certain secret pit which he himself had prepared for just such an emergency. That pit was in that house and was known probably to one person alone; in it he hid so continuously for one month that he hardly dared leave it to provide for his human needs. Food, when it was given to him, he ate in the secrecy of the pit, and every service was rendered to him by stealth. Praying, he prayed always with a torrent of tears that the Lord would deliver him from the hands of those who were persecuting his soul; ...and though he was in a pit and in darkness, he was nevertheless filled with a certain exquisite joy of which till then he had had no experience; and catching fire therefrom, he left the pit and exposed himself openly to the curses of his persecutors. [1Cel 10]

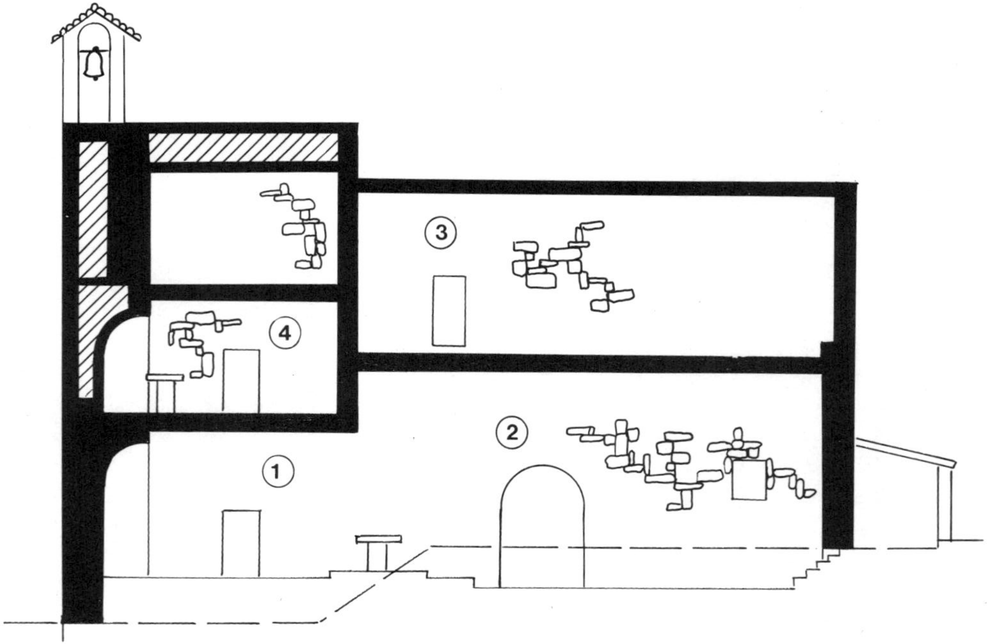

San Damiano after Francis

1. Sanctuary
2. Nave
3. Dormitory
4. Oratory

After Francis left his sacred hiding place and made a public renunciation of his father and his inheritance, he began to rebuild the old church of San Damiano which was in ruins. The renovating activity had a developmental impact upon Francis' life. He was given impetus to restore other dilapidated churches until his thought evolved into the consciousness that Christ wanted the spiritual edifice of the Church renewed.

San Damiano was under the jurisdiction of the Assisi diocese, hence, Bishop Guido. The bishop provided the ecclesiastical permission in 1212 for San Damiano to become the monastery for the Poor Ladies; Clare and Agnes moved in after a short time at Sant'Angelo.

The communal space that Clare developed as abbess and that sheltered the contemplative community was made up of mainly four areas: the choir, dormitory, infirmary and refectory:

> Let her [the Abbess] preserve common life in everything, especially in whatever pertains to the church, the dormitory, refectory, infirmary.... [RCl IV, 13]

It is believed that Francis' rebuilding of the ancient church included the construction of the dormitory over the church. For safety precautions, it was necessary for religious women to sleep in second floor dormitories accessible by rope ladders which were drawn up inside a bolted door at night. Infirm Sisters at the San Damiano monastery had a special place on second floor over the refectory.

Francis returned to spend some time at San Damiano after receiving the Stigmata--twelve years after Clare had begun the

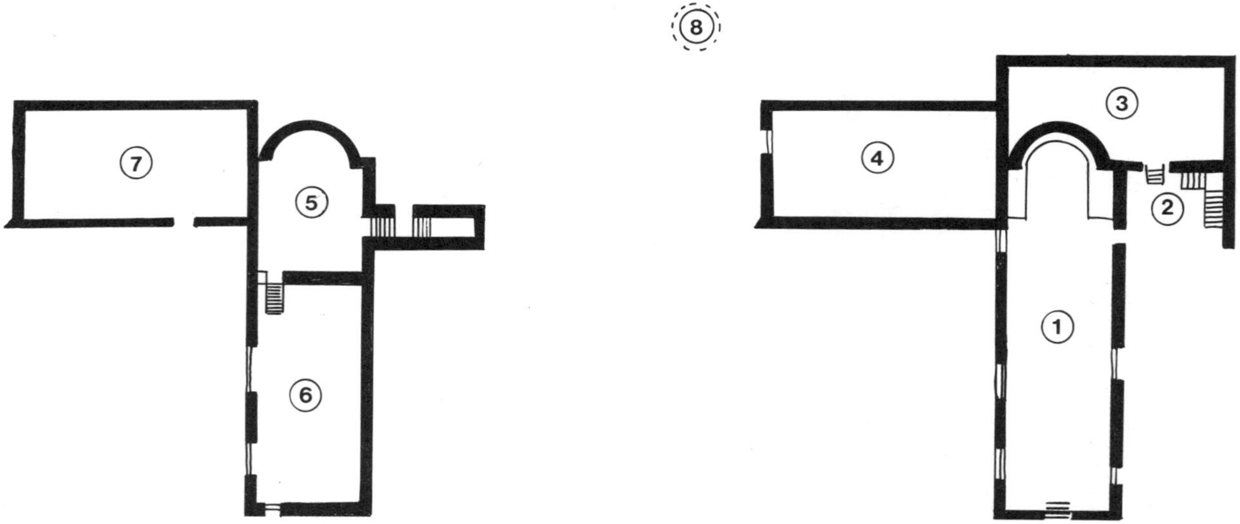

Monastery of the Poor Ladies

1. Church
2. Burial Vault
3. Choir
4. Refectory
5. Oratory
6. Dormitory
7. Infirmary
8. Well of S. Clare

community there. Perhaps he stayed in the original chaplain's hut, the residence for the canon who was there before Francis rebuilt San Damiano. The chaplain's hut stood near the apse of the church and quite close to the portion of the building that served as the refectory for the Poor Ladies. Here during the winter of 1224-25, he was inspired to write the "Canticle of Brother Sun." Also during this time, he composed the "Canticle of Exhortation to Saint Clare and Her Sisters":

> Listen, little poor ones called by the Lord, who have come together from many parts and provinces: Live always in truth, that you may die in obedience. Do not look at the life without, for that of the Spirit is better. I beg you through great love, to use with discretion the alms which the Lord gives you. Those who are weighed down by sickness and the others who are wearied because of them, all of you: bear it in peace. For you will sell this fatigue at a very high price and each one [of you] will be crowned queen in heaven with the Virgin Mary.

Francis died at the Portiuncula. The funeral procession carrying his body from there up into Assisi paused at San Damiano so that Clare and the Poor Ladies could view Francis and express their grief:

> They paused there [San Damiano], and the little window--through which the servants of Christ were accustomed to receive the sacrament of the Body of the Lord at the appointed time--was opened. The coffin was opened, in which a treasure of supercelestial virtues lay hidden and

in which he who was accustomed to bear many was being borne by a few. Behold, the Lady Clare, who was the first mother of the others since she was the very first plant of this holy Order, came with the rest of her daughters to see their father who would no longer speak to them or return to them for he was hastening elsewhere.

Redoubling their sighs and looking upon him with great sorrow of heart and many tears, they began to proclaim in a restrained voice: "Father, father, what shall we do? Why do you abandon us in our misery? or to whom do you leave us who are so desolate? Why did you not send us rejoicing ahead of you to the place where you are going--us whom you leave in prison, us whom you will never again visit as you used to?"

[1Cel 116]

When Clare died, her Sisters collaborated with Alexander IV for their move to San Giorgio where Clare's body was placed. Friars took up residence at San Damiano within a few years after the departure of the Sisters; records indicate that San Damiano belonged to the Sacro Convento in 1307. When the Observant movement was in its early stages, San Damiano was named in 1383 as one of the first ten convents under the direction of Paul d'Trinci. It continued its reputation for a more ascetical lifestyle and stricter observance of the Rule when it passed into the control of the Riformati in 1604.

The Italian government took over San Damiano--and all convents in Italy--during the Reunification of Italy. The property was purchased in 1897 by the Marquis of Ripon who turned it over to the friars for their use with the stipulation that there could not be any renovation done to the historic complex. September 22, 1983, dates the donation of the title of the property back to the Friars Minor.

Today, when we stand in front of the church of San Damiano, we can observe from the stone formation on the facade of the church that the friars doubled the width of the facade. During the sixteenth century the front portico was constructed with three arcades. The chapel to the right, which now serves as an entryway to the ancient church, is dedicated to St. Jerome. We walk through it to the chapel of the crucifix where we view a wooden crucifix carved by Friar Innocent of Palermo in the first half of the seventeenth century.

The sacred space of San Damiano offers us various niches for remembering Francis and Clare whose lives direct us to God. We can examine the window sill in the old church where the money was flung that a young Francis brought to the priest after selling a horse and cloth in Foligno. We can view the choir and places of prayer of Clare. Throughout the complex, we can experience the long standing tradition of San Damiano as a harbor to souls seeking God; a tradition that is continued in its interprovincial novitiate program and in its outreach ministry to youth and all pilgrims who come to "seek the Lord."

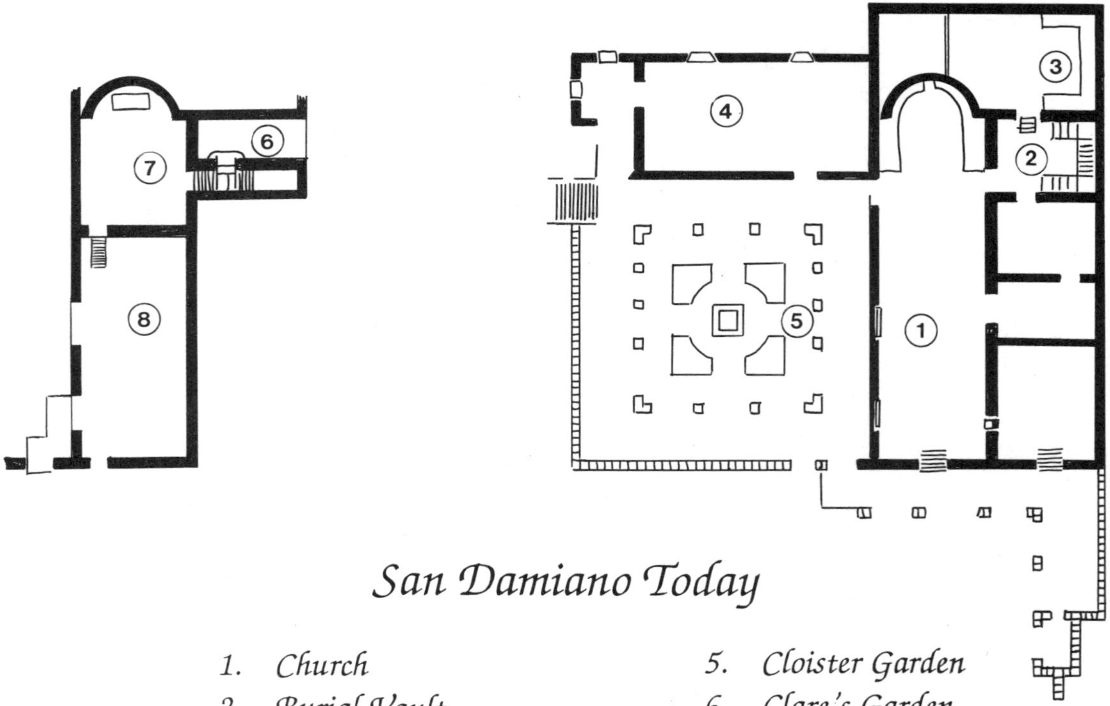

San Damiano Today

1. Church
2. Burial Vault
3. Choir
4. Refectory
5. Cloister Garden
6. Clare's Garden
7. Oratory of S. Clare
8. Dormitory

Further Reflection

Clare sought out the enclosed garden at San Damiano for privacy with her Beloved. There, she became the garden to whom the Beloved came (cf. Song of Songs 4:16-5:1). The natural beauty observable at San Damiano on the southern slope of the hill beneath Assisi mirrored the inward beauty of Clare's love. She clothed herself with the blossoms of virtues as she encouraged Agnes of Prague to do:

> Adorn yourself within and without with beautiful robes, covered, as is becoming the daughter and most chaste bride of the Most High King, with the flowers and garments of all the virtues. [4LAg 16-17]

The cross that spoke to Francis was at San Damiano throughout Clare's life. Clare prayed before the cross; she gazed, considered and contemplated the mystery of God's love beckoning her into the fullness of the Trinitarian life. Gazing at the icon drew her beyond Jesus into the fountainhead of Love, the source of all life, the Creator. Her womanly gaze stirred up her interior affection of a daughter for a parent, the compassion of a mother for her child and the unconditional love for her spouse, the Holy Spirit. She shared her self-understanding of her relationship with God in her letters to Agnes: "You have truly merited to be called a sister, spouse and mother of the Son of the Most High Father and of the glorious Virgin (1LAg 24)."

Life at San Damiano was a pilgrimage of poverty; the journey progressed from poverty to humility to charity climaxed in mysticism. Poverty embraced out of desire to follow in the footsteps of Our Lord Jesus Christ moved the will to desire humble obedience in the manner of the humility of Jesus:

> Who, though he was in the form of God, did not regard equality with God something to be grasped. Rather, he emptied himself, taking the form of a slave, coming in human likeness; and found human in appearance, he humbled himself, becoming obedient to death, even death on a cross. [Phil.2:6-8]

Clare pondered the mystery of the Incarnation--the King of heaven and earth whom the whole world could not contain chose to abide in the enclosure of Mary's womb (cf. 3LAg 18-19). She wrote to Agnes:

> Indeed, it is now clear that the soul of a faithful person, the most worthy of all creatures because of the grace of God, is greater than heaven itself, since the heavens and the rest of creation cannot contain their Creator and only the faithful soul is His dwelling place and throne, and this only through the charity that the wicked lack.
> [3LAg 21-22]

The intensity of Clare's love for the Incarnation was not withheld from her Sisters. One day at prayer, according to Sister Francesca, God's presence was made manifest:

> She [Francesca] saw in the lap of Saint Clare, before her breast, a young boy who was so beautiful that he could not be described. The same witness, because she saw that young boy, felt an indescribable sweetness and believed without a doubt he was the Son of God.
> [Proc IX,4]

The presence of the Child Jesus was made visible in the choir of the monastery at San Damiano by the unremitting gaze of Clare on her Beloved and the Beloved on Clare. Not only in the choir, but throughout the monastery, Jesus was made present by the unity of love that the Sisters had for one another. Clare understood that it was important for the community to live in love to know God. At the end of her life she wrote:

> Let all who hold offices in the monastery be chosen by the common consent of all the sisters to preserve the unity of mutual love and peace. [RCl IV,22]

How is our love for Our Lord Jesus Christ made visible in our homes?

Suggested Reading:

Armstrong, Regis J.. "Clare of Assisi: Mirror Mystic." *Cord* 35/7 (1985): 195-202.

Beha, Marie. "So Where Are We?" *Cord* 35/6 (1985): 164-70.

Bigaroni, Marino. "San Damiano - Assisi: The First Church of St. Francis." *Franciscan Studies* 47 (1987): 45-97.

Vaughn, John, and Lanfranco Serrini, Flavio Roberto Carraro and Jose' Angulo Quilis. "St. Clare: The Eight Hundredth Anniversary of Her Death." *Greyfriars Review* 6/2 (1992): 141-187.

Mortuary Chapel of San Giorgio

San Giorgio

Clare's presence at San Giorgio

The death of Clare initiated great celebration because everyone proclaimed her a saint. Crowds of persons assembled at San Damiano the day following her death to celebrate her funeral and to accompany her body to its place of rest at San Giorgio:

> The Cardinal priests then gathered with devout respect for the holy funeral and completed the customary rites over the body of the virgin. Finally, because they did not judge it safe or fitting to leave such a precious trust so far from the citizens, they carried it with hymns and [songs of] praise, the sound of trumpets and solemn rejoicing, and brought it honorably to San Giorgio. This is also the site where the body of the holy Father Francis had been buried so that he who had prepared the way of life while she lived also prepared--as if by foreknowledge--the place for her death. Afterwards, a gathering of many peoples came to the tomb of the virgin praising God and saying: "Truly holy, truly gloriously, she reigns with the angels, she who has received such honor from all on earth." [LegCl, 48]

Clare's holiness was proclaimed throughout the country. Two blind men at Narni had heard the fame of a "certain woman who recently died in Assisi and that the hand of the Lord is said to honor her grave with gifts of healing and many miracles [LegCl 52)]." They told their companion, Iacobello, about this source for healing. Iacobello hurried to Assisi where he received a restoration of his sight when he humbly touched Clare's tomb.

One of many accounts of healing that took place at Clare's grave is that of Giacomino:

> A certain boy of Perugia, Giacomino, seemed not so much to be sick as to be possessed by a very evil demon. In fact, he would at times throw himself desperately in the fire or hurl himself on the ground or bite stones until he had broken his teeth or...
>
> His father Giudolotto... turned to the merits of Saint Clare. "O most holy virgin," he said, "O Clare, honored by the world, I entrust my pitiable son to you and, with every prayer, I beg you for his cure."
>
> He hurried to the tomb filled with faith, brought the boy, and placed him on her grave. While he prayed, he immediately obtained her help. For the boy was at once free from that illness and never again afflicted by an injury of this kind. [LegCl 50]

Giacomino was one of many children whom Clare healed, even while she lived at San Damiano. Sister Benvenuta remembered the story of a young boy brought to the monastery from Spoleto:

> Mattiolo, three or four years old, had put a small pebble up one of the nostrils of his nose, so it could in no way be extricated. The young boy seemed to be in danger. After he was brought to Saint Clare and she made the sign of the cross over him, that pebble immediately fell from his nose. The young boy was cured. [Proc II, 18]

Sister Amata described the healing of a young boy from Perugia that both Clare and her mother ministered to:

> She said that a young boy from Perugia had a certain film over his eye which covered all of it. Then he was brought to Saint Clare who touched the eyes of the boy and then made the sign of the cross over him. Then she said: "Bring him to my mother, Sister Ortulana (who was in the monastery of San Damiano) and let her make the sign of the cross over him." After this had been done, the young boy was cured, so that Saint Clare said her mother had cured him. On the contrary, though, her mother said Lady Clare, her daughter, had cured him. Thus each one attributed this grace to the other.
> [Proc IV, 11]

There seems to be consistent evidence that Clare's healing touch was known by parents who were distraught with sick children. Once Lord Giovanni di Maestro Giovanni of Assisi carried his suffering son to Lady Clare. The boy had a fever and suffered with a scrofula. "The saint made the sign of the cross over him, touched him, and so cured him" [Proc IX,6]. Less than two years after Clare's death, her *Bull for Canonization* proclaimed:

> In truth, because a great and splendid light cannot be restrained from displaying the brilliance of its rays, the power of holiness shone in her life through many and various miracles. [BC, 14]

Historical Background

Medieval documents refer to the crossroads of San Giorgio outside the city walls of Assisi. There, on a knoll of the hillside, was situated a complex of buildings--the parish church of San Giorgio, the parochial school administered by the canons of the Cathedral of San Rufino and a hospice for sick pilgrims, refugees or epidemic victims [plague patients were kept outside the city walls as a preventive measure against further contagion]. The legend of St. George, and especially the account of the slaying of the dragon, was retold annually at the church on the saint's feast day, April 23rd. Such a tale inflamed the aspirations of young men for knighthood. The most famous student from San Giorgio school was St. Francis. He had outfitted himself as a knight and, in such a manner, was on his way to Apulia when his life's direction changed.

> [Francis] went to bed; but, half asleep, he heard a voice calling and asking him whither he was bound. He replied, telling of his plan. Then he, who had previously appeared to him in sleep, spoke these words: "Who do you think can best reward you, the Master or the

servant?" "The Master," answered Francis. "Then why do you leave the Master for the servant, the rich Lord for the poor man?" [L3S 6]

From then on Francis' loyalty was given to Our Lord Jesus Christ whom he followed unreservedly. When Francis and his early companions received papal approbation for their way of life, Francis "first began to preach where as a child he had first learned to read and where for a time he was buried amid great honor" [1Cel.23]. Pope Gregory IX canonized Francis in 1228 at San Giorgio where his body lay resting until his basilica was prepared for the transferral of his remains on May 25, 1230.

When Clare died, Pope Innocent IV presided over her funeral at San Damiano which concluded with a processional carrying of Clare's body to the crypt at San Giorgio where St. Francis' body had lain before 1230. The longtime friend and Cardinal Protector of the Poor Ladies, Cardinal Raynaldus, was elected to the papacy when Innocent IV died on December 12, 1254. He took the name Alexander IV and within a year canonized Clare on August 15, 1255, at Anagni. The *Bull of Canonization* for Clare offered a plenary indulgence to those who would visit her tomb on August 12th. Her date on the liturgical calendar was assigned to the 12th, the day after she died, because August 11th is the date set aside for Assisi's first bishop, St. Rufino.

Alexander IV exercised papal influence and arranged for the property of the San Giorgio complex to be given up by the canons of the Cathedral for the Basilica of Saint Clare and a residence for the Sisters from San Damiano. He decreed in 1259 that the few Sisters at San Giorgio with St. Clare's body and those still residing at San Damiano would be all united in one monastery under one abbess. All of the Poor Ladies from the original Poor Clare monastery at San Damiano moved by 1260 to the monastery built on the site of the complex surrounding San Giorgio. By that time, the old church of San Giorgio was reconstructed for the choir of the Poor Ladies. Their simple living quarters and choir leaned against the south side of the new basilica

Today, the Poor Clare community lives in an expanded monastery that extends south of the Basilica of Saint Clare and is built around an inner courtyard. In the courtyard, the Sisters have a hermitage whose origin goes back to the time of the San Giorgio complex. The small building could have been a mortuary chapel for the San Giorgio hospital. There, the Poor Clares reverence a cloth with blood stains from Francis' stigmatized body.

Further Reflection

Jesus' departing message to his disciples contains the promise that healings would continue in His name:

> These signs will accompany those who believe: in my name they will drive out demons, they will speak new languages. They will pick up serpents [with their hands], and if they drink any deadly thing, it will not harm them. They will lay hands on the sick, and they will recover.
>
> [Mark 16:17-18]

Clare's commitment to follow in the footsteps of Jesus shaped her compassionate heart. She extended such care to others that they were healed of their afflictions. The simplest malady, such as a heavy heart from bearing the frustrations of a day's trouble, was healed by Clare's tenderness:

> She wished that those whom she perceived unable to observe the common rigor be content to govern themselves with gentleness. If a temptation disturbed someone, if sadness took hold of someone, as is natural, she called her in secret and consoled her with tears. Sometimes she would place herself at the feet of the depressed [sister] so that she might relieve the force of [her] sadness with her motherly caresses. [LegCl 38]

Many Sisters who lived at San Damiano recounted their personal experiences of Clare's gift of healing. They consistently recalled that healing occurred after Clare made the sign of the cross over the person. Clare's faith and its accompanying healing power became known beyond San Damiano and persons came there for Clare's ministry. Even Francis referred persons to Clare:

> Because he knew of her great perfection and respected the great power in her, Blessed Francis sent to the Lady Clare a certain brother Stephen [who was] afflicted with madness in order that she might make the sign of the holy Cross over him. The daughter of obedience made the sign over him at the command of her Father and permitted him to sleep for a short while in the place where she was accustomed to pray. But that [brother], after being refreshed by a little sleep, got up healed, and returned to the Father, freed from his insanity.
>
> [LegCl 32]

The Legend of Clare states that the "Tree of the Cross was planted in the breast of the virgin...while its fruit refreshes the soul." Clare's compassion for her Sisters was such that she tried to teach them in the love of God to be sensitive toward the good for both the body and the soul. Sister Amata recalled that Clare asked God to heal "if it was best for the soul":

> Asked what the saint had said, she replied that after placing her hand over her, she asked God, if it were best for her soul, to cure her from these illnesses. She was instantly cured. [Proc IV,7]

Clare offers all contemporary Christians a paradigm for holiness. The transformation of her person was such that she took on the spirit of Jesus in reaching out to others. She embodied the love of Jesus so that the same healing power of the historical Jesus was transferred through her to others. The living faith of Clare extended the reign of God's love in her monastery and to those who came to her for help. Is this not the model for all Christians? The self-image is transformed until the authentic prayer arises from the heart, "It is no longer I who live, but it is Christ who lives in me" (Gal.2:20). Clare expressed confidently that she would continue to extend God's blessing to those who asked:

> I bless you during my life and after my death, as I am able, out of all the blessings with which the Father of mercies has and does bless His sons and daughters in heaven and on earth. [BCl 11]

When Clare was canonized within two years of her death, the *Bull of Canonization* proclaimed that through Clare "obvious remedies are felt here on earth":

> O Clare,
> endowed with so many brilliant titles!
> Bright even before your conversion,
> brighter in your manner of living,
> even brighter in your enclosed life,
> and brilliant in splendor after the course of your mortal life!
> In this Clare,
> a clear mirror of example has been given to this world;
> by this Clare, the sweet lily of virginity is offered among the heavenly delights;
> through this Clare,
> obvious remedies are felt here on earth.
>
> [BC 3]

How might Clare teach us to live the Christian life more confidently?

Suggested Reading:

Bigaroni, Marino. "La Chiesa di S. Giorgio in Assisi." *Archivum Franciscanum Historicum* 83 (1990): 3-49.

Basilica of Saint Clare

BASILICA OF SAINT CLARE

Historical Background

On October 3, 1260, the body of Saint Clare was transferred from its resting place in the Church of San Giorgio to the burial vault beneath the high altar of the newly completed basilica. After Clare's canonization in 1255, Pope Alexander IV provided papal leadership for the building of Saint Clare's basilica that there might be a proper place for pilgrims traveling to the tomb of this holy woman and a residence for Clare's Sisters close to their mother. The church was begun in 1257, completed in 1260 and consecrated in 1265. The cruciform design of the floor plan resembles the upper level of the basilica of St. Francis and the tall campanile attracts attention from afar. The facade has a beautiful rose window with four concentric circles. We can appreciate the window best if we enter the church during the afternoon when the sun from the western sky radiates through its design.

In order for the body of Saint Clare to be placed under the high altar in 1260, a passage was prepared from the rear of the Church slanting down fifteen feet to the spot where a small stone tomb had been constructed. It is not certain whether her body was

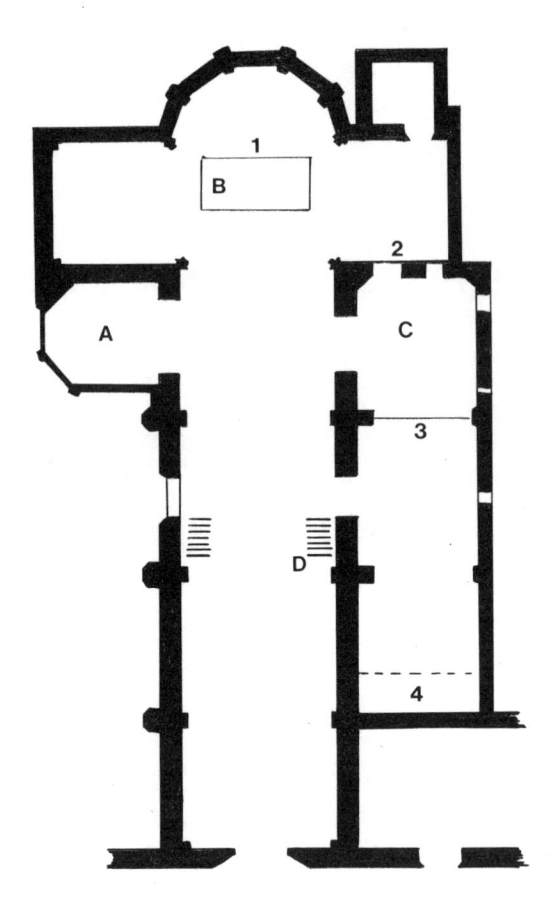

Basilica of Saint Clare

A. Chapel of S. Agnes
B. Main Altar
C. Blessed Sacrament Chapel
D. Stairway to the Crypt

1. Icon of the Crucified Christ
2. Dossal
3. San Damiano Cross
4. Relics

exhumed from the former tomb in the San Giorgio chapel or carried to its final resting place in the original coffin. When the coffin was opened in 1850, the saint's body lay before the viewers with one hand on the breast and the other hand lying at her side.

The side chapel of St. Agnes (Clare's sister) is the burial place for Agnes, Ortulana, Clare's mother, and Bl. Benedetta, the abbess who was Clare's successor. Moving past the chapel into the left transept, we discover two sacred images of the Mother of God, the Byzantine painting above the side altar and the Nativity scene fresco on the north wall. These contrasting images remind us that God is both transcendent and immanent, other-worldly and God-with-us.

The large icon of the Crucified Christ that hangs above the high altar was commissioned by Bl. Benedetta for that place of worship. Both Francis and Clare are seen kissing the bleeding feet of Christ while Benedetta, who is depicted as much smaller, looks on. Four ceiling vaults above the high altar portray holy women adoring God with the angels: 1) Mary, Mother of God, with St. Clare, 2) St. Agnes, martyr, and St. Agnes of Assisi, 3) Saints Catherine of Alexandria and Margaret and 4) Saints Lucy and Cecilia. The symbolic placement of these four pairs of women above the main altar proclaims that God is honored and glorified by the spiritual fruition from virginity. Mary of Nazareth is the prototype for all virgins. Her unflinching "yes" to God was repeated by the early virgin martyrs. These saints inspired a new type of medieval heroism lived by Clare and her followers. Clare and Agnes of Assisi renounced marriage and their noble inheritance for the daily suffering of following in the footsteps of the Poor Christ.

The 1283 pictorial biography of Clare, a dossal, hangs above the side altar in the right transept. This painting, completed only thirty years after Clare's death, conveys the popular cult recognizing Clare as both a saint and a foundress of a religious order. The style of the Giotto cycle for Francis is utilized here with episodes from Clare's life depicted in a clockwise pattern beginning on the lower left:

- the bishop hands Clare a palm [LegCl, 7]
- Francis welcomes Clare at the Portiuncula [LegCl, 7-8]
- Clare's investiture ceremony [LegCl, 8]
- Clare resists her family's pleas to return [LegCl, 9]
- Agnes joins Clare at Sant'Angelo [LegCl, 25]

There are two pictures of Agnes: the upper right shows Francis cutting Agnes' hair in the chapel of Sant'Angelo and beneath that, the scene of Clare's prayer for Agnes' safety while she resisted the relatives who tried to drag her away.

- Clare blesses the bread which multiplies [LegCl, 15]
- The Blessed Virgin comes for Clare at her death [LegCl, 46]
- Pope and bishops celebrate Clare's funeral [LegCL, 47-48]

The Blessed Sacrament chapel, to the right of the nave, was built to accommodate the parishioners of San Giorgio parish whose place of worship was taken away when the basilica was built. A curtain behind the altar separates the Poor Clares from public view while permitting them to participate in the Liturgies offered in that chapel. Likewise, pilgrims praying in the Blessed Sacrament chapel may hear the nuns' voices chanting Liturgy of the Hours in their choir behind the curtain.

A glass wall separates the Blessed Sacrament chapel from the chapel of the San Damiano cross. When we kneel at prieudieus for veneration before the cross, we notice prayer cards containing Francis' own prayer in many languages:

> All-highest, glorious God, cast your light into the darkness of my heart. Give me right faith, a firm hope, perfect charity and profound humility, with wisdom and perception, O Lord, so that I may do what is truly your holy will. Amen.

We walk to the rear of the San Damiano icon chapel to find the reliquary room harboring treasures from Francis and Clare. We are fortunate if we arrive while a Poor Clare Sister describes what is observed: the breviary of St. Francis which Brother Leo turned over to the Poor Clares for safe keeping, the 1253 Bull from Innocent IV which approved Clare's Rule, an embroidered alb that Clare prepared for Francis, locks of Clare's hair, a hair shirt, a piece of veil, Clare's mantle in which was found her original Rule in 1893, a penitent's tunic from the 13th century believed to have been worn by Francis, and a slipper that Clare made for Francis' stigmatized feet.

A staircase near the entrance to the reliquary chapel leads down to the crypt where Clare's body may be venerated. The discovery of Clare's body is celebrated on September 23rd. Her sarcophagus safely buried beneath the high altar in 1260 was opened in 1850 on September 23. When the coffin was opened on that date, it was discovered that her body remained intact. A new crypt chapel was constructed, completed in 1872, so that her body could be viewed by all pilgrims seeking her intercession. Clare's body exposed to public viewing eventually showed serious signs of deterioration and the decision was made to encase her body in a ceramic mold. The body was removed from viewing in November, 1986, and replaced with the present form in April, 1987. Today, we can view Clare resting in a simple glass coffin with her head on an olive wood pillow.

Further Reflection

Clare more than appreciated good preaching: she expected it. She sought for preachers to proclaim the Word of God and to provide instruction which would nourish the spiritual life of the Sisters. According to Sister Agnes, it was a known fact that Clare delighted in hearing the Word of God proclaimed:

> Lady Clare delighted in hearing the Word of God. Although she had never studied letters, she nevertheless listened willingly to learned sermons. [Proc X,8]

It is said that she was selective about what she took from a sermon:

> ...she believed that a nucleus lay hidden in the text that she would subtly perceive and enjoy with relish. She knew what to take out of the sermon of any preacher that might be profitable to the soul. [LegCl 37]

The conviction that the women at the San Damiano monastery needed inspiring preaching to sustain them in their contemplative lives was demonstrated in Clare's threat of a food boycott:

> Once when the Lord Pope Gregory forbade any brother to go to the monasteries of the Ladies without permission, the pious mother, sorrowing that her sisters would more rarely have the food of sacred teaching, sighed: "Let him now take away from us all the brothers since he has taken away those who provide us with the food that is vital." At once she sent back to the minister all the brothers, not wanting to have the questors who acquired corporal bread when they could not have the questors for spiritual bread. When Pope Gregory heard this, he immediately mitigated that prohibition into the hands of the general minister. [LegCl 37]

Contemplating the Word of God gave Clare such enthusiasm for God that her Sisters looked forward to her returning to them from prayer time so that they could reap learnings from her:

> When she came from prayer, she admonished and comforted her sisters, always speaking the words of God Who was always in her mouth, so much so that she did not want to speak of vanities. When she returned from her prayer, the sisters rejoiced as though she had come from heaven. [Proc I,9]

The psalmist prayed, "Your Word is a lamp to guide me, and a light for my path"(Ps. 119: 105). The testimony of the witnesses regarding the radiance of Clare during and after prayer reveals that her love of the Word of God offered her direction and consolation on her life's journey. Clare, who knew that there would always be a light for the path, encouraged her sisters to perseverance:

> Let us be very careful, therefore, that if we have set out on the path of the Lord, we do not at any time turn away from it through our own fault or negligence or ignorance, nor that we offend so great a Lord and His Virgin Mother, and our blessed father Francis.   [Test 74 - 75]

How might we grow in appreciation of the Word of God?

Suggested Readings

Bartoli, Marco. *Clare of Assisi.* Trans. Sr. Frances Teresa. Quincy, IL: Franciscan Press, 1993.

ASSISI

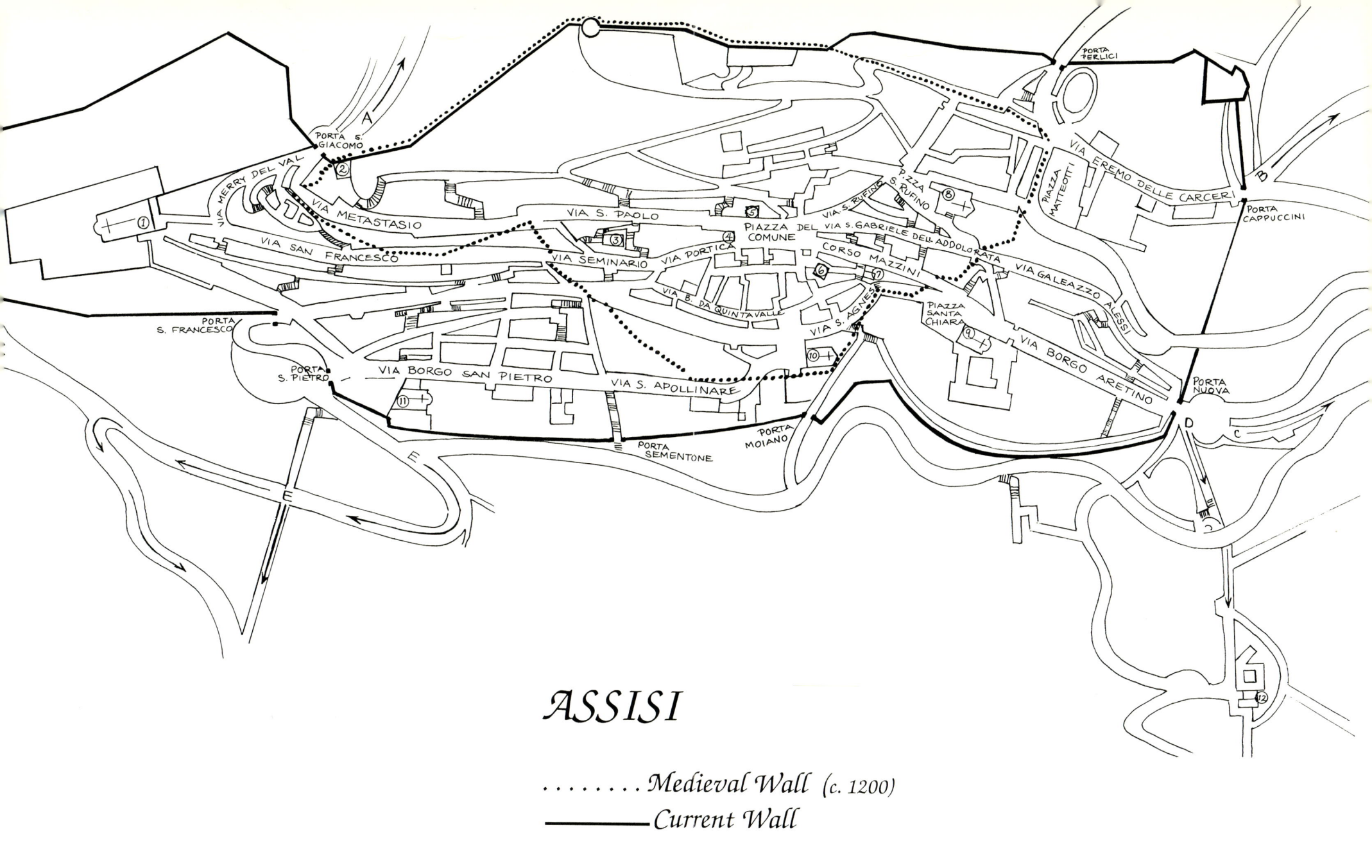

········ Medieval Wall (c. 1200)
─── Current Wall

1. Basilica of S. Francesco
2. S. Giacomo de Muro Rupto
3. S. Stefano
4. S. Niccolo
5. Temple of Minerva
6. Chiesa Nuova
7. Oratory of S. Francesco Piccolo
8. Cathedral of San Rufino
9. Basilica of S. Chiara
10. S. Maria Maggiore
11. S. Pietro
12. San Damiano

A → Cemetery
B → Carceri
C → Panzo
D → San Damiano
E → Portiuncula

Umbrian Valley
Medieval Times

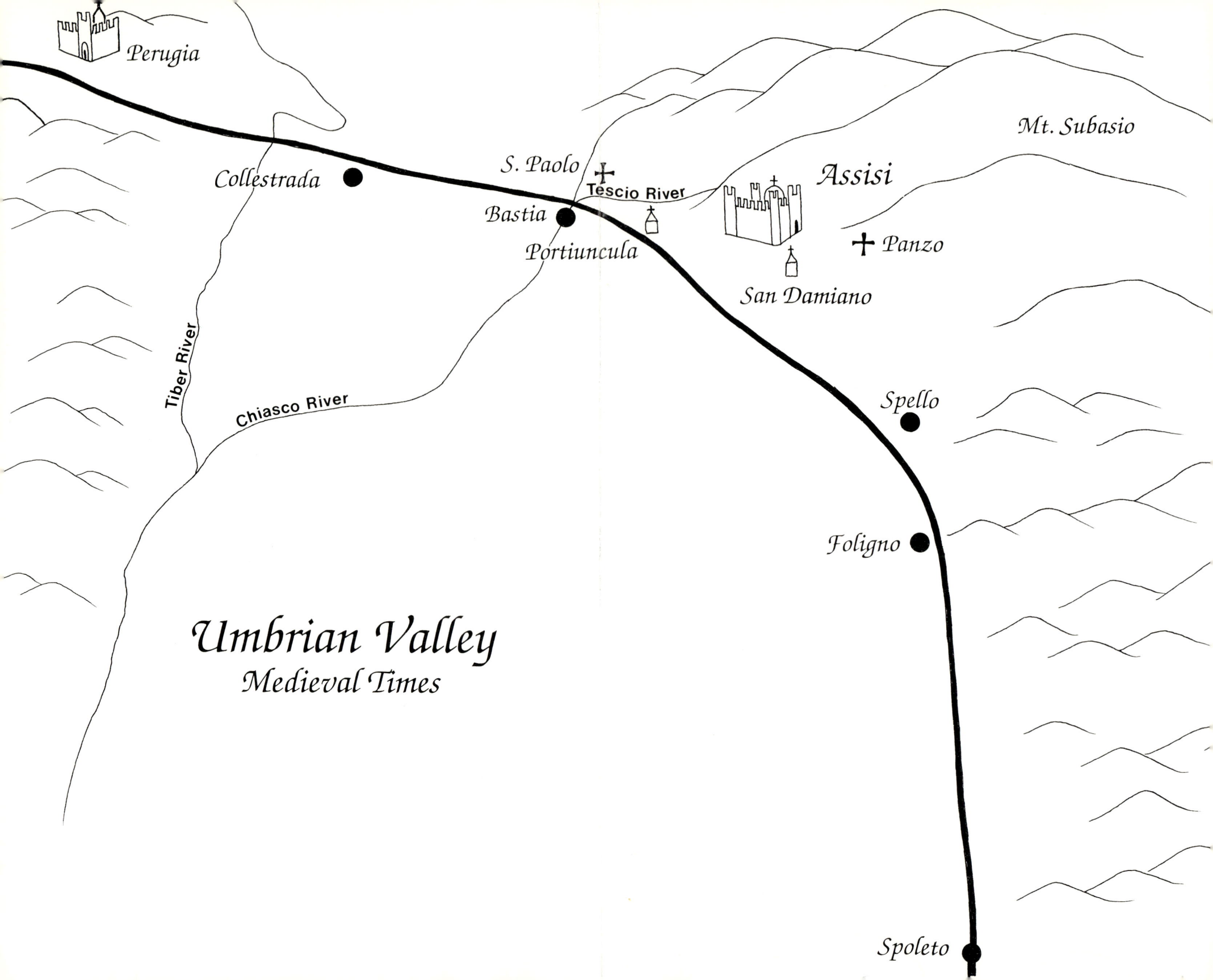

- Perugia
- Collestrada
- S. Paolo
- Tescio River
- Bastia
- Portiuncula
- Assisi
- Mt. Subasio
- Panzo
- San Damiano
- Spello
- Foligno
- Spoleto
- Tiber River
- Chiasco River